W9-ALV-875

"The book is fantastic. It is a readable, detailed, timely, step-by-step Social Security playbook. It helps readers master the Social Security game."

—Phyllis Bernstein, CPA/PFS
Former Director of Personal Financial
Planning for the American Institute of CPAs

"If you spend 60 minutes with this book, you may be able to increase your lifetime income from Social Security by tens of thousands or even hundreds of thousands of dollars."

—Paul Merriman, Author,
Financial Fitness Forever

"Get this book and read it now! It could save or make you an enormous amount of money."

—Brian Tracy, Author,
Make More Money

"This book is the real deal. It delivers crucial, timely information about the new Social Security rules with clarity and precision and should be required reading for everyone age 62 to 70 who is, or ever was, married."

—Elaine Floyd, CFP®, Author,
Savvy Social Security Planning for Boomers,
an advisor training program

"The number one goal for retiring and retired Baby Boomers is cash flow for what might be 2, 3 or more decades of post-retirement life. This book is a great, understandable and practical introduction to one key component of that later life cash flow, Social Security."

—Martin M. Shenkman, CPA, MBA, AEP, PFS, JD

"Read James Lange's excellent book and learn how and when to take your Social Security and retirement accounts. Doing so will pay for itself hundreds if not thousands of times over"

— Laurence Kotlikoff,
Boston University Economist,
Co-Author of ***Get What's Yours: The Revised Secrets***

*"Think of **Retire Secure!** as a GPS for your money. You may know where you are and where you want to go, but you don't know how to get there. Jim offers the best routes."*

*"**Retire Secure!** is a very practical investment guide on how to defer taxes and efficiently plan for retirement and your estate."*

*"**The Roth Revolution** is must reading for anyone contemplating moving money into a Roth IRA, which in my opinion is everyone. Jim Lange is one of the few people who has the knowledge when it comes to IRAs and also the ability to put this knowledge into understandable language."*

The

$214,000
MISTAKE

How to Double Your Social Security & Maximize Your IRAs

Proven Strategies for Couples Ages 62-70

James Lange, *CPA/Attorney*

The $214,000 Mistake

ISBN 978-0-9903588-7-9

Retire Secure Press
PayTaxesLater.com
412-521-2732
2200 Murray Ave.
Pittsburgh, PA 15217

Interior layout - MiniBük, MiniBuk.com
Manufactured by MiniBük®, a registered trademark of MiniBük, LLC
Typefaces: Franklin Gothic (Headlines), Utopia Std (Body Text)

Introduction

One of the reasons I wrote this book was to help married taxpayers get the most out of their Social Security benefits. Though estimates vary, as many as 97 percent of married Social Security recipients fail to optimize their benefits. A second reason, very directly related to the first, is that the failure to optimize Social Security benefits frequently imposes significant consequences on the wife who must go on after the death of her husband—statistically the greater probability.

The $214,000 difference referred to in the book title is shown in Figure 3, Single Person Starting Social Security Benefits (Age 62 vs. 70), on page 19.

All proceeds of this book go to charity: water, a non-profit organization bringing clean and safe drinking water to people in developing countries.

How Important Is It to Get the Right Strategies for Social Security and Roth IRA Conversions?

Let's take a quick look at two couples, the Rushers and the Planners who live next door to each other. They both have $1.1 million, identically invested, and they both want to spend $75,000 per year after they retire. But they differ in their ideas about Social Security and Roth IRA conversion strategies. Which neighbor will have more peace of mind throughout retirement? The assumptions used for figure 1 can be found on page 98.

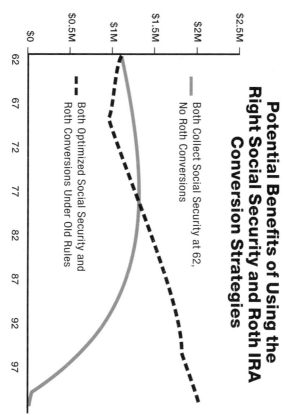

FIGURE 1:

Potential Benefits of Using the Right Social Security and Roth IRA Conversion Strategies

Net After-Tax Assets

Both Collect Social Security at 62, No Roth Conversions

Both Optimized Social Security and Roth Conversions Under Old Rules

As you can see, the Rushers' wealth (depicted by the solid line) will be higher while in their 70s, but they will have to start worrying about money in their 80s as they watch their portfolio dwindle. They'll have to cut their spending or else they'll run out of money if they live too long. The Planners (depicted by the dashed line), will notice a reduction in their assets from the time they are age 62 until they turn age 70. But after that, their wealth will climb, and they can look forward to the future with confidence knowing that they are financially secure. When the Rushers run out of money, the Planners will still have $2,013,881 in their portfolio. And remember, they began with identical portfolios. Why the life-changing difference? The Rushers began taking Social Security based on their respective earnings records at age 62, and they didn't make any Roth IRA conversions. The Planners optimized their Social Security strategies. Please note that both couples spent the same amount of money so it isn't a matter of living a reduced lifestyle between ages 62 to 70 so you can live it up at age 70. They took advantage of every Social Security strategy available, which made a significant difference in their annual income when they finally did receive their benefits. They also bit the bullet and paid the income tax due on a series of optimally timed Roth IRA conversions.

Optimizing Social Security and
Retirement Plan Options

The 2017 Tax Reform created enormous opportunity for many IRA and retirement plan owners by lowering their tax brackets. By applying the cutting-edge retirement strategies described in detail throughout this book, and at the appropriate time, you can maximize both your and your spouse's long-term Social Security income. This can help guarantee your financial security, and even a much stronger financial outlook for your heirs after you pass.

The strategies that are discussed in detail and displayed quantitatively in this book exemplify the reasons for delaying your application for Social Security benefits to age 70 to ensure that you receive the highest benefit possible. If you are married (were married, or filing for divorce), the opportunities and benefits of optimizing Social Security and IRA planning increase dramatically. With people living longer today (wives outliving their husbands by, on average, 7 years), delaying your application, particularly if you are married, can be a game-changer in retirement. It means you can boost your own Social Security benefits while you are alive, and maximize the benefit paid to the survivor – which, ultimately, is the most important goal. Your surviving spouse will be able to live her remaining years with greater financial confidence and security, knowing that she will receive a significantly higher income from Social Security for the rest of her life.

Have you have already made a bad decision by applying for Social Security early? If so, don't worry—I have some ideas that could make a significant difference in your retirement outlook. If you are single or divorced, these proven strategies can help you as well.

If you believe the tax reductions made in the 2017 Tax Reform are temporary, you might want to consider a series of Roth IRA Conversions sooner than later. A series of Roth IRA conversions executed in conjunction with optimal Social Security strategies is a powerful combination – particularly if you made several conversions over multiple years at lower tax rates. You don't even need to wait – you can take advantage of some of these techniques right now to keep the IRS' hands off your hard-earned retirement money and ensure that your heirs receive as much as is legally possible.

Table of Contents

Chapter 1 1
Why Coordinating Your Social Security and Roth IRA
Conversion Strategies Is Critically Important 1
  Why Trust Our Analysis? 12
  Whose Analysis Shouldn't You Trust? 14

Chapter 2 16
The Reasons You Should Delay Taking
Social Security Benefits 16
  How Your Benefit is Calculated 21
  When Should I Apply? 22
  Collecting Benefits While You're Working 28

Chapter 3 31
Social Security Options for Married Couples 31
  Married Couples Need to Think About
  Social Security as a Team 31

Chapter 4 42
Survivor Benefits – The Key to Financial Security for the
Surviving Spouse 42
  Receiving the Higher of Two Benefits 48

Chapter 5 51
Claim Now, Claim More Later –
One of the Last of the Loopholes 51
  Making the Strategy Work 53
  How the Strategy Will Work in 2020 56

Chapter 6 58
The Synergy of Roth Conversions and the Timing of
Social Security Benefits 58
  What is a Roth Conversion? 60
  Should You Convert? 60
  Why There is a Synergy between Optimizing Social
  Security and Roth IRA Conversions 64

Converting to a Roth While in
Your Lowest Tax Bracket 65

Chapter 7 70
What If I Have Already Made a Bad Decision? 70
What If I Am Already Receiving Social Security but I
Like the Idea of a Roth Conversion? 72

Chapter 8 74
Social Security for Divorcees and Singles 74
Single People 74
Divorced People 77

Chapter 9 81
Should the Question of Social Security's Solvency
Motivate Me to Take Benefits as Soon as I Can? 81

Conclusion and Summary 87

Appendix 89
Use These Tips When Applying for Benefits 89
The Application Process 90
Applying Online 90
Filing a Restricted Application
for Spousal Benefits 92
Finalizing Your Application 93
Applying by Telephone 94
Applying in Person at a Social
Security Administration Office 95
Which Way Is Best? 97

Assumptions 98

Additional Resources 101
7 More Ways We Can Help You
Get the Most Out of Your IRA 101
Everyone Needs a Good
Financial Game Plan 105
To inquire about a *Free Second Opinion* 109

CHAPTER 1

Why Coordinating Your Social Security and Roth IRA Conversion Strategies Is Critically Important

In the late 1960s, Stanford University conducted a series of studies on the value of delayed gratification. Researchers offered children a choice: they could have one marshmallow immediately, or if they waited 15 minutes, they could have two marshmallows. Most of the children couldn't wait and they immediately ate their one marshmallow. Some, however, waited the 15 minutes and got two marshmallows. They tracked those kids for 40 years and found that the children who were able to delay gratification had dramatically better outcomes in many areas of their later lives.

So, are you a one or two marshmallow person? Are you willing to consider making financial decisions that might make the short term seem a little less favorable, but the long-term outlook for your retirement a lot brighter? For example, how would you react if I asked you to consider not applying for your Social Security benefits as soon as you are permitted? What if I suggested that you purposely spend part of your savings to pay income taxes years before the IRS would require you to? What if I added a bit more incentive and told you that these strategies have become even more powerful since the passage in 2017 of the major tax overhaul known as the Tax Cuts and Jobs Act?

Discussing retirement and estate planning strategies with clients is a very significant part of my job, and I do believe it has to be a conversation—I can't simply issue directives. For instance, years ago, during one of these conversations, I recommended that my client hold off applying for Social Security until he was 70 and that he take advantage of the years that he wasn't collecting benefits to execute (and pay income tax on) a series of Roth IRA conversions. He was a retired engineer who thought he knew as much about financial strategies as he did about engineering. (It isn't a totally rare occurrence... but I have license to poke fun at engineers because my wife is a software engineer)!

He insisted that it wasn't the right strategy for him. He felt that he and his wife should both start taking Social Security at 62 and that they should completely avoid the additional income tax they'd owe if they executed Roth IRA conversions. He also told me that his biggest concern was that he and/or his wife would outlive their money.

With his biggest concern identified, I knew that if I could present compelling evidence that supported my point of view, using reasonable assumptions, he would at least consider an alternative plan.

I have worked with countless relatively stubborn, but quantitatively gifted clients. With this group, I have an ace up my sleeve. Most of them, especially the very bright ones, are data-driven. That means if you show them the math, the spreadsheets behind the math, the assumptions used on the spreadsheets and why I am recommending what I am recommending, their objections, at least for most of them, grudgingly diminish or even disappear.

Much to his surprise, I was able to prove to him that, even though my recommendations seemed counterintuitive, acting on them would allow both he and his wife to significantly reduce the chances of outliving their money and would even *increase* the amount of money they could safely spend. Each time I see him, he tells me how glad he and his wife are that I took the time to run the numbers and show him why his previous strategy was wrong. For them, it made a huge difference. And since they aren't big spenders themselves, taking my advice will ultimately make an enormous difference for their children and grandchildren.

We have "run the numbers" for thousands of clients who are considering Roth IRA conversions and comparing their Social Security options. And, while we use multiple software programs to run the calculations, the real skill that our CPA "number crunchers" bring to the table is deciding which numbers to include in our calculations. Roth IRA conversions and Social Security analysis account for only part of our calculations. We regularly factor in other variables as well, such as safe spending rates, rates-of-return, gifting programs, mortgage repayment, and pension distributions. Including a comprehensive analysis of those factors, however, is outside the scope of this book. Our highly qualified CPAs also crunch the numbers for our articles, many of which are published in prestigious peer-reviewed journals, as well as our books.

For a free copy of our Roth IRA conversion book, **The Roth Revolution***, go to* www.paytaxeslater.com/books*. For our video and audio version of this book, as well as other financial resources, go to* www.paytaxeslater.com/The214kMistake*.*

So, let's look at the numbers for this client.

We ran the numbers using three different scenarios based on the couple having $1.1 million in investments and spending $75,000 per year. The results are shown in Figure 2. The assumptions used for Figure 2 can be found on page 98

FIGURE 2:

Assets Available for Retirement Years

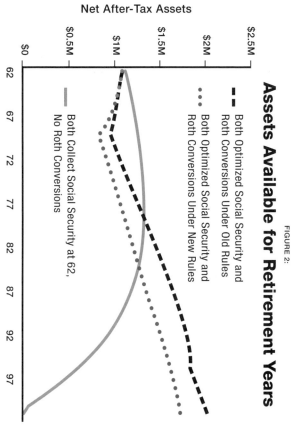

Net After-Tax Assets

- – – Both Optimized Social Security and Roth Conversions Under Old Rules
- · · · Both Optimized Social Security and Roth Conversions Under New Rules
- —— Both Collect Social Security at 62, No Roth Conversions

I never recommend that clients spend less money immediately after retirement to produce a larger income at age 70, so the spending assumptions are constant throughout their lifetimes.

The solid line shows the outcome they would have experienced if they'd acted on their original plan to take Social Security at age 62. In the early years of their retirement, they'd have had a little more money because of the Social Security income.

Just as many young adults don't think much about their retirement, many retirees in their 60s don't project where their finances will be in their 80s or 90s. So, take another look at the solid line. What are the consequences when they're age 80 because they decided to take Social Security early and not make any Roth IRA conversions? Inflation has caused their expenses to go up, but their wealth hasn't grown over the past decade, and now it's even starting to go the other direction! If they live long enough, they'll see a significant portion of their nest egg vanish. They will have to reduce expenses or face the possibility that they'll run out of money completely before they die. Their worst fear.

> *Just as many young adults don't think much about their retirement, many retirees in their 60s don't project where their finances will be in their 80s or 90s.*

Fortunately, my client was a data-driven, two-marshmallow guy. He dug into the spreadsheets we used to make our calculations. I think he was secretly hoping we had made a major error so he could prove us wrong, but he realized our calculations and advice were sound. Once persuaded, they took my advice regarding Social Security, and they took advantage of a strategy that is no longer available called "Apply and Suspend." And even though it was painful, they ate into their savings and paid income tax so that they could make a series of Roth IRA conversions.

But look at what happens when they turn 70. The outcome is represented by the dashed line. Those Social Security checks finally start to come in, and they're *a lot* bigger than they would have been if he'd taken them early. (I'll show you exactly how much bigger in Chapter 2). Those big checks allow them to rebuild their savings quickly and, by the time they're about 80, they're in a position similar to what they would have been if they had taken their Social Security early. *The difference, though, is that they can look forward to their remaining years with confidence.*

They will never run out of money and will likely leave a significant estate behind for their children. That financial security gives them peace of mind through their retirement years. They also know that, given our assumptions, they could have as much as $2,013,881 to pass on to their children after they die, compared to being broke if they had followed through with their original plan.

Unfortunately, new Social Security claimants will never be able to take advantage of that precise scenario because of a change in the rules. Not having the option to "Apply and Suspend" does have an impact on the overall outcome, and the result that new claimants might realize is depicted by the dotted line. Even though the dotted line represents the same Roth IRA conversion strategy, and uses the best Social Security strategies *currently* available, the change in the rules is costly. If we compare the two projections, using the new rules means that a new claimant, using an optimized strategy, will have $251,511 *less* by the time they turn age 82, than if they had been able to use Apply and Suspend. That is why I wrote a book and did a lot of Social Security workshops and radio shows in 2015. I wanted clients, readers, and listeners to take advantage of the Apply and Suspend rules while they still had the chance. Fortunately, the word got through to most of our clients and countless readers and listeners. Unfortunately, too many people, especially people with more modest portfolios, never got the news. Either they didn't know about us or the other experts advocating the same thing, or they didn't listen.

Social Security benefits aren't getting more generous – in fact, they're going the other way. The government has already eliminated several methods (they called them "loopholes") that you used to be able to use to get higher benefits. The Apply and Suspend strategy was one of these. I continue to refer to it in this book because many readers applied before the deadline under the old rules, and I don't want to cause any consternation among them by leading them to believe that their status has changed. But, even though the Social Security rules are not quite as favorable now as when my client in the example applied, you can clearly see that the decisions you make about your retirement can make the difference between living a comfortable lifestyle and running out of money.

> *Social Security benefits aren't getting more generous – in fact, they're going the other way.*

One of the arguments I occasionally hear is "Gee Jim, if I hold off until I am 70, I won't be able to live comfortably until then because I won't have enough money from my portfolio to support my lifestyle between ages 62 and 70." My response, though usually not well received, is that if you are 62 and you don't have enough savings or IRAs to live comfortably without having to rely on your Social Security for income, I would suggest that you don't have enough money to retire unless you are willing to live extremely frugally. Perhaps continuing to work for a few more years would be more prudent—I have had those conversations. Luckily, it is far more typical for me to prove to my clients that they can spend even more than they currently spend, using our recommendations.

But, what if you do have savings and/or an IRA but don't want to withdraw principal during your early years of retirement? Before we run the numbers, it is common for clients to feel uncomfortable with the idea of spending down their portfolio when they could just as easily take their Social Security early. They don't like delaying their Social Security and being forced to spend down their savings to maintain their regular spending patterns. That is precisely when having compelling proof from running the numbers is so critical: they see it is better to hold off taking their Social Security and continue to spend at their normal rate. This can be true even if you have no savings or after-tax dollars and you must take taxable distributions from your IRA to make up for the fact you are delaying your Social Security.

So, take another look at Figure 2. You can see that, given certain reasonable assumptions which are listed on Page 98 in this book, taking advantage of optimal strategies for Social Security and executing a series of Roth IRA conversions can make the difference between running out of money and having more than $1.5 million when you die (more than $2 million if you were able to use the old Apply and Suspend rules). And if you optimize your own situation by making good decisions, you can give your family financial security and pass the benefits on to your heirs.

Remember, each of the three scenarios reflects the same amount of money in investments, earning the same rate-of-return, with the same annual spending. The only differences in our scenario are due to two factors: which Social Security strategy they chose to use and whether they completed a series of Roth IRA conversions. Of course, like snowflakes, no two couples are the same. I go back to my earlier comment about "having a conversation, not issuing directives." When we run the numbers, the client is in the room and is part of the process. We don't ask clients to blindly trust us. Each situation must be evaluated according to its own facts and circumstances. But the basic facts are undisputed:

getting your Social Security strategy right and optimizing Roth IRA conversions can make an enormous difference to your and your family's financial future.

Why Trust Our Analysis?

You can rely on our analysis. We do extensive calculations before we offer advice, and our Social Security calculations have withstood the scrutiny of a panel of experts at one of the nation's most prestigious peer-reviewed magazines, **Trusts & Estates**. Our Roth IRA conversion analysis has withstood the close inspection of a panel of CPA tax experts and has been published in the tax journal of the American Institute of CPAs, **The Tax Adviser**.

Furthermore, I've interviewed some of the nation's top Social Security experts on my radio show, *The Lange Money Hour*. My guests have included Jane Bryant Quinn, who writes financial columns for **Newsweek**, **Bloomberg**, and AARP; Jonathan Clements, formerly the top personal finance writer for **The Wall Street Journal** for 18 years; Elaine Floyd, who is a nationally recognized Social Security and Roth IRA expert, and Mary Beth Franklin, who teaches courses on Social Security to financial professionals. One of my most thought-provoking guests was Larry Kotlikoff, who is the author of the # 1 best-selling book on Social Security: **Get What's Yours**. He believes that delaying your application for Social Security benefits to receive a higher guaranteed income for the rest of your and your spouse's life does not necessarily mean that you need to live frugally during your early retirement years – and I'll show you why I agree with him in Chapter 2.

> *Plan for the long term by implementing smart retirement strategies, which usually involves at least one member of the couple delaying their application for Social Security*

Our basic advice is consistent with what all these Social Security experts have said on our radio show: plan for the long term by implementing smart retirement strategies, which usually involves at least one member of the couple delaying their application for Social Security. The change in legislation that is explained thoroughly in this mini-book has made things much trickier for individuals who are trying to plan their retirement. Elaine Floyd said this about the current legislation: "Each couple's situation is different with regard to how the legislation will affect them. They need to come and see (us) so (we) can give them personalized guidance." The snowflake analogy holds true. In my own practice, I've found that there is no one-size-fits-all answer to the question about how to maximize Social Security benefits and Roth IRA conversions for a married couple. You must do the math and sometimes consider factors that are difficult to quantify before arriving at the best answer. That said, this mini-book offers a lot of guidance. You will see that combining the best possible Social Security options you have available, and using the optimal Roth IRA conversion strategies, can be a game changer for you and your family.

To listen to past guest speakers from **The Lange Money Hour: Where *Smart* Money Talks**, *go to* www.paytaxeslater.com/radio-show/guests. *From there you can hear from Jane Bryant Quinn, Jonathan Clements and other leading IRA, retirement planning and financial experts.*

I am currently writing a book on how to respond to the 2017 tax reform, which will dive deeper into Roth IRA conversions. For information regarding getting a free copy of that book, or any books listed, please go to www.paytaxeslater.com/books

Whose Analysis Shouldn't You Trust?

There are some sources that you should almost NEVER trust when it comes to getting information about Social Security. This includes your non-expert friends, and your local Social Security office. I lead many workshops on retirement planning. I can't tell you how many participants have come up and told me that they went to their local Social Security office and received and followed advice that is completely opposite to what I offer in my workshop. Even worse, they realized that following the advice they got from the Social Security office has cost them over $100,000! Of course, there are some knowledgeable people working for the Social Security offices, but they aren't sophisticated wealth advisors who can evaluate all aspects of your financial situation before they give you advice. Another questionable source of information is a financial professional who can't prove his advice is right. Statements such as "the government is going to screw you, so take the money now" is not sufficient proof to reduce one of your important safety nets. That said, it is critical to know that, even if you have failed to make the best decisions in the past, it doesn't necessarily mean you can't make a course correction now. Let's dig in!

CHAPTER 2

The Reasons You Should Delay Taking Social Security Benefits

Your decision about when to apply for Social Security benefits should not be based on the fear that you will die early. If you die young, you will be dead. You won't have any financial worries. Your fear should be that you will live a long time and outlive your money!

To introduce some of the complexities involved in Social Security decision making, I am going to start with the most straightforward example: an unmarried individual who is weighing whether to take his Social Security at age 62 or wait until later. Once we establish the basic analysis, I will address these same questions as they apply to married couples. If you are unmarried but in a committed relationship, the ideas presented in this and the following chapter should offer some serious food for thought. Expanding Social Security benefits is one of the primary financial advantages of getting married—I have an idea for a book, ***Get Married for the Money***, and it is only partly tongue-in-cheek.

I had another client, a 62-year-old unmarried gentleman who I will call Reluctant Robert. He was weighing the advantages of applying for Social Security at age 62 versus age 70. Reluctant Robert didn't trust the government, and he wanted his Social Security benefits immediately. First, he argued, if he didn't live until age 70, he'd never receive any money from Social Security — a complete waste of all his dutifully paid deductions. And second, even though he knew he would receive a higher benefit if he waited, he didn't believe the higher benefit would outpace, over the long term, the deficit engendered by waiting — even if he did live to a ripe old age. But was he correct?

We took Reluctant Robert through our paces. We told him that if he applied for benefits at age 62 and deposited every check he received into an account that earned 4 percent, which is a very generous rate of return for an account that guarantees his principal, he would have almost $288,524 in the bank on his 70th birthday. On the other hand, if he waited until age 70 to apply, he'd have received no money at all from Social Security. Money vs. no money. It's a no-brainer, right?

Then I showed Robert the peer-reviewed Figure 3 below, which demonstrates that, if he waits and then applies for the higher benefit at age 70, he'll have more money at age 83 than if he had started collecting at age 62. We wanted to compare apples to apples, so we assumed that, in both scenarios, Reluctant Robert banked his Social Security proceeds in an account that earned a 4 percent rate of return. I am being generous in assuming that Reluctant Robert could find a safe investment at 4 percent. If the investment earns closer to 1 or 2 percent, which is closer to the guaranteed rates of return available from banks at the time this book was written, the advantage of waiting would be considerably greater and the breakeven point even earlier. It wouldn't be realistic to do a comparison where Reluctant Robert receives more than 4 percent because Social Security increases are guaranteed, and I don't think any legitimate advisor would say you could get better than 4 percent guaranteed these days. So, let's take a look at what I showed him. The assumptions used for Figure 3 can be found on Page 99.

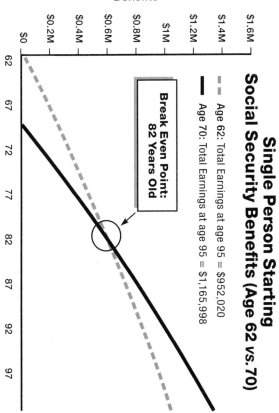

FIGURE 3:

Single Person Starting
Social Security Benefits (Age 62 vs. 70)

- - - Age 62: Total Earnings at age 95 = $952,020

—— Age 70: Total Earnings at age 95 = $1,165,998

Break Even Point: 82 Years Old

Reluctant Robert was still grumbling. The early years look pretty bad. He's paid into the system for years and until the day he turns 70, he will not have gotten a dime out of it. His golfing buddies will be laughing at him because they have been collecting checks for years. But look at what happens when he turns 70 and he does get his first check. It's a lot higher than the one he'd have gotten if he'd signed up at age 62. If Reluctant Robert had gone with his gut instinct and started taking benefits at age 62, he would be receiving monthly payments of $2,790 which, because of Cost of Living Adjustments (COLAs), would increase to $3,480 by the time he is age 70. If he listens to our advice and waits until age 70 to apply, he will receive $5,635 per month plus COLAs. That's a difference of $2,155 every month, or an annual increase in benefits of $25,860 plus COLAs for the rest of his life! If he lives until age 95, the higher benefit earned by waiting means a difference of $213,798! Robert just couldn't believe it. In other words, in many cases you can double your Social Security benefit by waiting until you are 70 to start collecting.

For virtually all my current and prospective clients, getting Social Security right is important, but it is even more important for individuals with fewer financial resources. When I give Social Security workshops, I aggressively give my books to the hotel staff. Many of those employees might benefit from the information even more than many of the attendees. I don't know if any of them read the book, but I hope some do. If you are reading this book, chances are that you probably have a substantial portfolio. But, it is individuals without a substantial portfolio who will experience an even greater difference in their lifestyles than my typical reader, if they follow our Social Security recommendations.

> *In other words, in many cases you can double your Social Security benefit by waiting until you are 70 to start collecting.*

How Your Benefit is Calculated

The amount of Social Security that you can expect to receive will depend on several factors. These include:

- how much you earned over your working career, and when you earned it
- your marital status
- the age at which you apply for benefits
- and the strategy (or strategies) that you use to claim them – which I'll discuss in detail later in this book

The Social Security Administration periodically mails a statement that estimates your retirement benefit, but it is best to access it online at ssa.gov/mystatement. The Social Security website, ssa.gov, has some other interesting features that you can also use. You can click on the button that says, "Estimate Your Retirement Benefit." You can also access their planning calculators by using this link: ssa.gov/planners/benefitcalculators.htm. Larry Kotlikoff offers an excellent free calculator at basic.esplanner.com. You can also upgrade to a paid version that provides some incredibly powerful features for "do-it-yourself" readers.

When Should I Apply?

I told Robert that deciding when to apply for Social Security benefits might be one of the most important financial decisions he would ever make. In our financial advisory practice, we review all the options available to our clients before they file for benefits. If they have already filed, we still review their available options because sometimes they can make changes that will allow them to get a higher Social Security benefit later by stopping their benefit now, or in some cases even giving the money back! Of course, we love it when readers get the strategy right from the beginning, but sometimes a course correction can also make a significant difference.

The age at which you can receive full benefits is determined by the year you were born, and it is called your Full Retirement Age (FRA). If you were born earlier than 1943, you have already reached your FRA. If you were born between 1943 and 1954, you will reach your FRA when you turn 66. If you were born in 1955 or later, your FRA will be greater than age 66.

Let's assume that you were born between 1943 and 1954 and that your FRA is 66. If you wait to apply for benefits at age 66, you will receive what is called your Primary Insurance Amount (PIA). You are permitted to apply for benefits before you turn 66 but if you do, it will cost you. If you apply at age 62, for example, your monthly benefit will be reduced by *25 percent*. You will also forego the Cost of Living Adjustments (COLAs) that would have been applied to the 25 percent you won't receive because you applied early.

What does that reduction mean in terms of dollars and cents? If your PIA is $2,000 and you apply for Social Security benefits at age 62 instead of your FRA of 66, the 25 percent penalty means that your benefit will be *reduced* by $500 every month, for the rest of your life. Over twelve months, that's $6,000— and that doesn't include the cost of living increases you're missing out on. Over ten years, you will have missed out on $60,000 (not including COLAs) for the simple reason that you applied for Social Security benefits four years before your FRA. Now are you starting to understand why I told Reluctant Robert to not apply for Social Security when he became eligible at age 62? In his case, the penalty that he would have received by applying before his FRA would have cost him dearly.

This news is even worse for you baby boomers. If you were born in 1955 or later, your FRA is even greater than age 66. So, let's suppose that you were born in 1955. If so, your FRA is 66 plus 2 months, and the penalty you will receive for applying at age 62 is even costlier than 25 percent. By filing for benefits at 62, you didn't just apply four years early – you applied four years and two months too early! And the later that you were born, the higher the penalty for applying for benefits before your FRA. If your FRA is 67 (born in 1960 or later), the penalty for applying at age 62 is a whopping *30 percent*.

Back to readers born between 1943 and 1954. If you wait beyond your Full Retirement Age to apply, your monthly benefit will be *increased* by 8 percent for every year you wait, up until you turn 70. The increase in benefit you receive because you waited is called a Delayed Retirement Credit (DRC). It is like getting two marshmallows because you didn't eat the first one when you had the chance. Your benefit also earns COLAs, like a bonus chocolate bar that you can melt and eat with your marshmallow when you are 70, even though you aren't receiving a check right now. If you get your Roth IRA conversions right, you get another bonus, graham crackers. For the purposes of this book, we will refer to the DRCs as 8 percent annual "raises" that you can earn if you wait to apply for benefits even after your Full Retirement Age.

What do the DRCs mean in terms of dollars and cents? If your PIA at your FRA of 66 is $2,000 and you wait until age 70 to apply, Social Security will give you those DRCs (or raises) and increase your benefit by at least 8 percent every year. And if you wait four years, that's a 32 percent increase – so you'll get (at least) $2,640 every month, for the rest of your life. (Your benefit amount is also increased for COLAs, but to keep the math simple, this example only shows how the DRCs work). That's (at least) $7,680 more every year, *and* it's guaranteed for the rest of your life. Over ten years, that's at least $76,800 more than you would have received if you applied at your FRA.

So, let's return to Reluctant Robert. He was 62 and had three basic options available to him. He could apply for benefits at 62, be penalized, AND lose out on his raises—for which he would receive $18,000 ($1,500 x 12) every year. Or he could wait until age 66 to apply and get $24,000 ($2,000 x 12) every year – avoiding the penalty, but still losing out on his raises. Or he could wait until 70 to apply and get $31,680 ($2,640 x 12) every year – avoiding the penalty and earning 8 percent raises for four years. (Note, these are conservative estimates, because to keep the math simple, I did not include COLAs that would also be applied).

But still, Reluctant Robert was skeptical. He understood the math but told me that both of his parents had died at age 80 and that he wasn't sure he would live long enough to make the strategy pay off. Well, if he dies before age 82, then yes, looking only at the numbers, it would have been a bad decision. But, Larry Kotlikoff, a Boston University economist, and one of the country's leading experts on Social Security, exposed the weakness in Robert's thinking, and in his opinion, the misguided priorities. And this is one of the most important concepts in this book: *If you (and your spouse, if you are married) die early, you will have no financial problems because you will be dead (maybe a bit harsh, but true). What you should be worried about is that you (and/or your spouse) will outlive your savings.* So, when I told that to Reluctant Robert, he agreed that he would be very, very happy if he had a large government-guaranteed check coming in each month if he did live beyond age 82. (Note: this higher guaranteed income is even more important for married couples, and I'll show you why later in this book).

> *If you (and your spouse, if you are married)*
> *die early, you will have no financial problems*
> *because you will be dead (maybe a bit harsh,*
> *but true). What you should be worried about*
> *is that you (and/or your spouse) will outlive*
> *your savings.*

Here's another thing that I knew instinctively but Larry Kotlikoff articulated it as well as I have ever heard. If you want to hold off on applying for Social Security, you don't have to spend your early years of retirement living frugally. While you are waiting to collect, you can still spend the exact same amount of money as if you were collecting benefits. Let me explain. Let's assume your benefit at age 66 is $3,000/month, but you elect to wait until age 70 to apply because it will increase to $4,528/month if you get those DRCs and COLAs. You can still spend $3,000 every month at 66 even if you don't collect your Social Security then. In order to do so, though, you will have to dip into your portfolio — an idea that seems anathema to most people! They think they should hang on to their portfolios for as long as possible because they want to have a nest egg they can spend in their later years. The fear of dipping into the portfolio increases if the entire portfolio is made up of IRA and retirement plan money that will trigger taxes upon withdrawal. But those are false fears that could cause you to make the wrong decision with your Social Security strategy. The additional income you will receive from Social Security by waiting will more than compensate for dipping into your portfolio, even if your portfolio consists of nothing but IRAs. I don't want you to live like a pauper in your early retirement because you are holding up on your Social Security so that you can live it up at 70. The idea is to be able to spend as much or more now, and still be guaranteed a higher income for the rest of your and your spouse's lives. For a thorough discussion of this point, we recommend Larry Kotlikoff's book, *Spend 'til The End*.

> *If you want to hold off on applying for Social Security, you don't have to spend your early years of retirement living frugally.*

To listen to past episodes of Larry Kotlikoff, Ph.D. guest speak on **The Lange Money Hour: Where** *Smart* **Money Talks***, visit this link* www.paytaxeslater.com/radio-show/guests/larry-kotlikoff.

Collecting Benefits While You're Working
If you continue to work, you should know how the Social Security benefits you are entitled to receive can be affected by wage income.

Let's take the worst case scenario and assume that you are working, but want to apply for Social Security because you need additional income. If you are under FRA and exceed an established earned income limit ($17,040 in 2018), your Social Security benefit will be reduced by $1 for every $2 you earn in excess of the limit. Unfortunately, this incentivizes some individuals to make up to $17,040, but no more because they don't want their Social Security income reduced.

Here's an example. Suppose you file for benefits at age 62 and your payment is $1,000 per month (or $12,000 per year), but you also plan to work and earn $24,000. That's $6,960 over the 2018 income limit of $17,040. Social Security will reduce your benefit by $3,480 (or $1 for every $2 you earn over the income limit) from your benefit. So even though you might think that you're going to get $12,000 from Social Security that year, you'll only get $8,520! I didn't want you to retire at 62 and start collecting Social Security in the first place – and I certainly don't want you to realize that you made a mistake and go back to work, only to find out that your benefits will be reduced because of your wage income!

Don't confuse this reduction with the tax that you may owe on your benefit! Depending on your income from other sources, as much as 85 percent of your income from Social Security will be taxed. The rate at which it is taxed, of course, depends on the tax bracket that you are in.

If you are FRA or older, there is no reduction in your benefit for working no matter how much you earn while working. That in itself isn't a good enough reason to apply for Social Security benefits while you are still working! Recognizing the optimal age at which to apply for benefits is a big decision that should not be taken lightly. And the decision is even more important for married couples.

> *Recognizing the optimal age at which to apply for benefits is a big decision that should not be taken lightly.*

CHAPTER 3

Social Security Options for Married Couples

Married couples should understand that, subject to rare exceptions, the spouse with the strongest earnings should wait until age 70 before applying for Social Security benefits. I can't stress that enough.

> *It is critical — essential even — to consider not only your own income needs but also the needs of your spouse during your lifetime and after your death.*

Married Couples Need to Think About Social Security as a Team

The decisions and choices you make when applying for Social Security will have a direct effect on the benefits that your spouse will receive while you are alive and after your death. Therefore, it is critical—essential even—to consider not only your own income needs but also the needs of your spouse during your lifetime and after your death. In this chapter, we will look at the effects of your decisions while you are both alive and what happens after one partner dies, which is perhaps even more critical.

Let's consider, for the moment, the basics of long-term financial planning for married couples. Virtually all my clients who are married say their first goal is to ensure the financial security (as well as the health and happiness) of both spouses while they are alive. The second goal is to make sure the surviving spouse is still protected after the first spouse dies. For many couples, the best way to accomplish both goals is for the individual with the stronger earnings record to wait until age 70 to apply for benefits. Why? To answer that question, you need to understand how spousal benefits and survivor benefits work. Just for the record, *spousal benefits* are different from the benefit that Social Security pays to a surviving spouse – I address the critical issue of *survivor benefits* in the next chapter.

Spousal benefits allow you to apply for benefits based on your spouse's earnings record. But there are some rules.

1. The primary earner must currently be receiving retirement or disability benefits for the spouse to be eligible for a spousal benefit.
2. The spouse claiming a spousal benefit must be at least age 62.
3. Generally, the couple has to have been married for at least one year.

So, if you are married and your spouse has applied for Social Security benefits, you may be able to file for benefits based on your spouse's earnings record. That can be valuable if your spouse was the higher wage earner. If you wait until your Full Retirement Age (FRA) to apply for spousal benefits, you will receive one-half (50 percent) of your spouse's Primary Insurance Amount (PIA). (If you're divorced, you might even be eligible to receive spousal benefits on your ex's record – but those are different rules that I'll cover in Chapter 8).

> *If you are married and your spouse has applied for Social Security benefits, you may be able to file for benefits based on your spouse's earnings record.*

In times of inflation and rising prices, Social Security benefits are also increased by COLAs. There have been years when the economy has stagnated and Social Security recipients have not had their checks increased by COLAs. But if COLAs are awarded, they are applied to spousal benefits as well as the primary earners' benefit. For the moment, let's look at a simple example that does not account for COLAs.

Over the course of their marriage, John worked outside the home and Jane did not. She stayed home to raise their children. Now, at ages 62, they are dreaming about the day when John can retire and would like to know when it will be financially possible. John's Social Security statement indicates that his PIA at his FRA of 66 is $3,000 per month. Jane has no earnings record of her own but will be eligible to apply for spousal benefits based on John's record. If she waits until her own FRA of 66 to apply for benefits, Jane's spousal benefit will be $1,500 (50 percent of John's PIA). Therefore, if they both wait until FRA to start taking benefits, they will have an income of $4,500 per month.

Just out of curiosity, let's look at what would happen if Jane applied for spousal benefits before her FRA. It's not good news. For every month in advance of her FRA that she applies, Social Security will permanently reduce her benefit. If Jane applies for spousal benefits at age 63, 36 months before her FRA, she'd only get $1,125 per month – or 37.5 percent of John's benefit. If she applies at age 62, she'd get even less – only 35 percent of John's benefit, or $1,050.

Now, let's look at what happens if John, fundamentally a two-marshmallow person, waits until age 70 to receive his benefits. Note that, under the new rules, this delays Jane's ability to apply for spousal benefits until she is age 70 (because in this example they are both the same age).

By age 70, John's PIA of $3,000 will be multiplied by those 8 percent raises for four years (plus COLAs, which for simplicity's sake I'm not accounting for here), which increases his benefit to $3,960 every month. Jane's spousal benefit at age 70 would be $1,500 (50 percent of John's PIA).

Wait a minute. What? Didn't I just say that Jane's spousal benefit would be $1,500 if she and John both applied at age 66? And now I'm also saying that Jane's spousal benefit would be $1,500 if they both waited until age 70 to apply? That can't be correct!

Unfortunately, it is. Do you remember when I said earlier that Social Security benefits aren't getting any more generous and, in fact, are going in the other direction? Poor Jane is feeling the effects of that first hand. Her spousal benefit will not be increased by John's 8 percent raises if she waits until age 70 to apply. And, because of the change in the rules, Jane *can't collect spousal benefits until John applies for his own benefit.* Under the old "apply and suspend" rules, John would have been allowed to *apply* for and then *suspend* his benefits. That in turn, would have allowed Jane to collect spousal benefits from ages 66 to 70. At which point, John, at age 70, would begin to receive his higher benefits increased by those 8 percent raises!

Figure 4 shows the difference in John and Jane's outlook if they both apply for Social Security benefits as soon as they are eligible at age 62, if they both apply at 66, or if they wait and both apply at age 70. The assumptions I used in Figure 4 can be found on Page 99 of this book.

James Lange

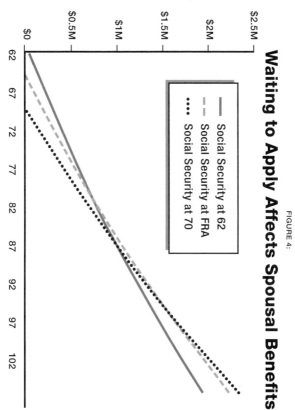

Accumulated Social Security Benefits

Waiting to Apply Affects Spousal Benefits

FIGURE 4:

—— Social Security at 62

– – Social Security at FRA

•••• Social Security at 70

And I can hear the outcry already. "The difference between applying at age 66 vs. age 70 is miniscule! I'm going to take my money and run!"

Before you march down to your local Social Security office with your papers in hand, I want to point out two things. First, there is a *significant* difference in their wealth during retirement if both John and Jane apply at 62 (the solid line), compared to applying at age 70 (the dotted line). But quite honestly, my first concern isn't about giving you a better lifestyle while you're both living. I'm more worried about making sure that the survivor has enough money to live on after one of you dies. So, if you think that that difference shown in Figure 4 above isn't enough to justify waiting until 70, then I think you need to read the next chapter when I show what happens if John dies and Jane is left on her own. That is where you will finally see why it so important for the primary earner to wait to file.

Now, let's change the scenario. After years of raising the kids, Jane takes a job working outside of the home. Based on her personal earnings record, Jane's Social Security statement indicates that her PIA at FRA is $900. The Social Security statement also compares her benefit based on her own earnings record with the benefit she is eligible to receive as a spousal benefit. In this example, Jane's spousal benefit ($1,500) is higher than her own benefit, so

Social Security will calculate a "spousal add-on," which means that she will receive an amount equal to her spousal benefit. What if Jane's own benefit was higher than the spousal benefit she's entitled to? Then, she receives her own benefit because it is higher.

The Bipartisan Budget Act of 2015 took much of the guesswork out of filing for spousal benefits. Since the new law took effect, individuals who turned 62 after January 2, 2016 are automatically "deemed" to be filing for every benefit they're entitled to. So, for most of the people reading this book now, your application will be fairly straightforward. When you file, Social Security will compare your own benefit to any spousal benefit to which you might be entitled and give you an amount equal to the highest benefit.

> *The Bipartisan Budget Act of 2015 took much of the guesswork out of filing for spousal benefits.*

As of this writing, there remains one exception to the general rule about applying for spousal benefits, and that would be to file a "Restricted Application for benefits." It is a way to get more money from Social Security, but it is on its way out too—courtesy of the Bipartisan Budget Act of 2015. It simply has a longer phase-out period than Apply and Suspend did. In order to file a Restricted Application for benefits, you had to have been born on or before December 31, 1953, and your spouse must either be collecting benefits now or filed an application to Apply and Suspend benefits under the old rules. If this is you, please read Chapter 5 closely, because you might be able to collect up to $60,000 in additional benefits if you qualify.

Now, I know there are going to be readers sputtering at my insistence that claimants cannot collect spousal benefits unless their spouse is also collecting his or her benefits. "My Aunt Edna is collecting spousal benefits while her husband, Uncle Herbert, (the primary earner) is not yet collecting his. Why are you telling me I can't do that too?" Luckily for Edna and Herbert, they are taking advantage of one of the Social Security "loopholes" that the government eliminated for new applicants in 2016—unfortunately for the rest of us. So, unless you were born in the right years and followed the advice in our last edition and submitted an application for the Apply and Suspend technique by the deadline, you're too late to take advantage of it.

Now that you've seen just how much of a difference your decisions about when and how to take Social Security will affect you during your retirement, while you are both living, please read on. Those decisions will become even more critical after the death of your spouse.

> *In order to file a Restricted Application for benefits, you had to have been born on or before December 31, 1953, and your spouse must either be collecting benefits now or filed an application to Apply and Suspend benefits under the old rules.*

*For a free copy of our Roth IRA conversion book, **The Roth Revolution**, go to* www.paytaxeslater.com/books. *For our video and audio version of this book, as well as other financial resources, go to* www.paytaxeslater.com/The214kMistake.

CHAPTER 4

Survivor Benefits – The Key to Financial Security for the Surviving Spouse

What happens to a couple's Social Security benefits after one of you dies? You lose one Social Security check, and your household income decreases. That is why it's important to make smart decisions while you are both alive and evaluating your options. When one of you dies, you want the survivor to receive as much guaranteed income from Social Security as possible.

Let's return to our example of John and Jane. We'll begin with the worst-case scenario. They didn't take my advice to wait as long as possible to apply for Social Security benefits and jumped on the bandwagon at ages 62. John's full retirement age is 66 as is Jane's.

Because he applies at age 62, four years before his FRA, John's benefit is reduced by 25%. So, instead of getting $3,000 every month (which would be his PIA at age 66), he'll get $2,250 ($3,000 x 0.75 = $2,250).

Jane pays an even steeper price for applying early. If she waits until age 66, her benefit will be $1,500 (50% of John's PIA at his FRA). But, at age 62, she will receive only 32.5% of John's PIA at FRA, or $975 ($3,000 x 0.325 = $975). So, beginning at age 62, their total monthly income from Social Security is $3,225. (Once again, to demonstrate the concept simply, we are not including COLAs that would have been added).

What happens if John dies at age 66? His monthly benefit check stops. Jane will lose her monthly spousal benefit, but she will receive a survivor benefit instead. Since Jane is at FRA, also age 66, she will receive, as her survivor benefit, either the amount that John had been collecting ($2,250) or 82.5% of his PIA ($3,000), whichever is higher. In this example, the latter amount is higher.

Now, we look at the best-case scenario. John and Jane take my advice to heart and wait until they are 70-years-old to begin taking benefits. Jane receives her full spousal benefit of $1,500 (one-half of John's primary insurance amount of $3,000). And, because John waited an additional four years after his FRA (age 66), he receives four years of Delayed Retirement Credits (DRCs) that have increased his benefit by 8 percent every year – making his government-guaranteed check $3,960 every month. Their monthly household income from Social Security is $5,460. (These are very conservative estimates because it assumes that no COLAs were added to their checks. If COLAs are granted, those amounts would be even higher). But here is the bottom line: The difference between applying as soon as they are eligible and waiting until they are required to receive benefits means a difference of at least $25,920 in their Social Security income every year!

Believe it or not, holding out for more money isn't the most important reason for delaying your Social Security application—especially if you are the primary earner. It is the survivor benefit that is most important. Let's assume that John delays taking his Social Security until age 70, and then he dies at age 71. What happens to this couple then? Poor John never really got to see much benefit of waiting until age 70 to apply for his Social Security, but Jane will be very, very glad that he did. Because, after John's death, Jane will receive a survivor benefit equal to John's higher benefit amount for the rest of her life.

> *Believe it or not, holding out for more money isn't the most important reason for delaying your Social Security application—especially if you are the primary earner. It is the survivor benefit that is most important.*

The idea of Jane receiving the higher survivor benefit amount might sound good at first, but remember, that this household will only receive one Social Security check from now on. That's right –

Jane's spousal benefit will stop when she switches to John's survivor benefit. Prior to John's death, they received $65,520 ($3,960 x 12 + $1,500 x 12) every year from Social Security, and now Jane will receive only $47,520 ($3,960 x 12) – a 37 percent reduction in the household annual income from Social Security.

But Jane was lucky because John waited to apply. If he had applied at age 62, her survivor benefit would only be $2,457 every month – or $29,700 every year. Figure 5 below shows the difference that Social Security can make in Jane's income during her golden years if John waits until age 70 to apply for his own benefit:

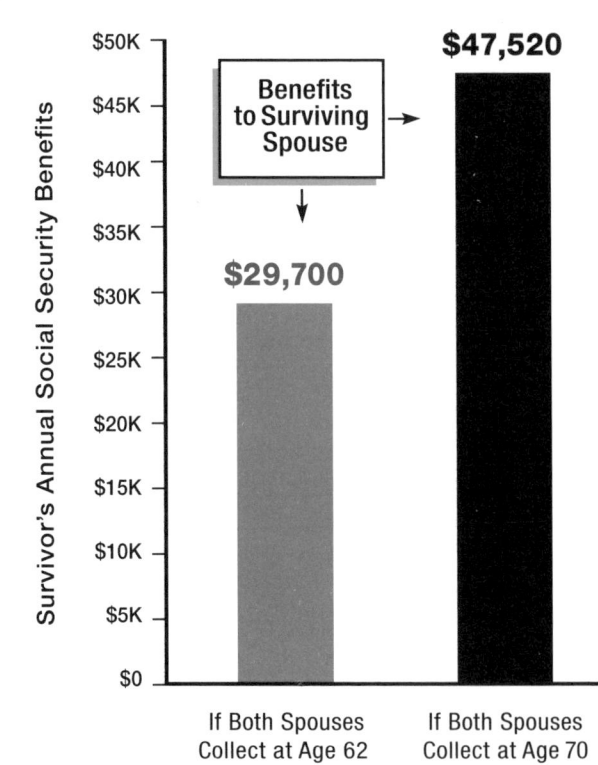

Income Stream for the Survivor

$47,520

Benefits
to Surviving
Spouse →

↓

$29,700

Survivor's Annual Social Security Benefits

$50K
$45K
$40K
$35K
$30K
$25K
$20K
$15K
$10K
$5K
$0

If Both Spouses
Collect at Age 62

If Both Spouses
Collect at Age 70

Figure 5 shows you why it is so important to plan your Social Security strategy well – after the first spouse dies, the survivor will have a much higher income every year, and it is guaranteed for the rest of his or her life! Of course, the $47,520 is higher than today's maximum benefit of $33,456, but these are projections for the future.

The death of a spouse can be financially as well as emotionally devastating, especially if there is a lengthy illness and the cost of medical care depletes the family's savings. What if this had been the case with John, and Jane had no other resources to live on after his death? Social Security will allow her to apply for survivor benefits as early as age 60, but the rules for doing so are so complicated that they are well beyond the scope of this little book. In most instances, you really shouldn't consider doing it unless you have absolutely no other alternatives than to set up a tent under a bridge and live there.

> *The death of a spouse can be financially as well as emotionally devastating, especially if there is a lengthy illness and the cost of medical care depletes the family's savings.*

Receiving the Higher of Two Benefits

Understanding that the surviving spouse will receive only the higher of the two benefits is extremely important. If the spouse with the stronger earnings record waits until at least age 66, or better yet age 70, to collect benefits, the survivor benefit will be enhanced. This is a crucial bit of knowledge when considering strategies to maximize your income from Social Security.

The amount of the survivor benefit will depend on the age at which the deceased spouse originally claimed his or her benefit, and the age at which the surviving spouse claims the survivor benefit. And since the financial goal for most couples is to guarantee the highest income for both spouses' lives, it is a good strategy to ensure that at least one of the spouses receives a Social Security benefit that is as high as possible. Obviously, most of us don't know when we will die! But, as we said at the beginning of the book, it makes more sense to prepare, as best we can, for a long life of financial security.

Let's look at another example.

Bill, the primary worker of the married couple, is 66, but he suffers from a serious heart condition and estimates his life expectancy is 5 years. His wife, also 66, is in excellent health and expects to live well into her nineties. She never worked outside of the home. How can the couple make the best of a tough situation? Bill should not collect Social Security benefits when he is 66-years-old, i.e., now. He should wait until he is 70-years-old so that his benefit will be increased by the 8 percent raises (DRCs) and COLAs every year for the 4 years between ages 66 and 70. Why? Because that course of action will provide his wife with greater financial security after his death. She will receive a survivor's benefit that will be 32 percent (plus the COLAs) higher for the rest of her life.

> *Since the financial goal for most couples is to guarantee the highest income for both spouses' lives, it is a good strategy to ensure that at least one of the spouses receives a Social Security benefit that is as high as possible.*

Even if Bill's health prognosis was better, just knowing the survivor benefit will be the higher of the two benefits should influence his decision. Statistics show that, in general, women live longer than men. Social Security says that a woman turning 65 today can expect to live until age 86.6. If there is a bigger difference in ages between a husband and his younger wife, a larger survivor benefit will be especially valuable—she could be living a long time after her husband dies.

Men who were the primary earners during their marriages who take their Social Security benefits early are not only hurting themselves but to a greater degree are hurting their wives. And even though the "loopholes" for spousal benefits that existed under the Social Security system in years past have closed or are in the process of closing, there are still options available to you that can provide a significantly higher guaranteed benefit for both you and your spouse, for the rest of your lives — if you know how to take advantage of them.

CHAPTER 5

Claim Now, Claim More Later –
One of the Last of the Loopholes

One of the last remaining loopholes involves filing a Restricted Application for benefits, but is also known as the Claim Now, Claim More Later strategy. As you saw in Chapter 2, most married individuals are eligible to collect benefits based on their own record as well as their spouse's record. Restricting your application means that you are applying for only one of the Social Security benefits for which you might be eligible. Then at some point in the future, you can change your filing and apply for a different type of benefit.

This strategy will be eliminated at the end of 2019 by the Bipartisan Budget Act of 2015 but, if you qualify for it, it can help you get more money from your spousal benefits. If you qualify and file a Restricted Application for benefits while the option is still available, you will receive benefits under the old rules even after the rules change. The spouse who wants to file the Restricted Application for benefits must have been born on or before December 31, 1953. If that's not you, you can skip this chapter completely because the strategy will be eliminated by the time you're old enough to apply for it.

> *If you qualify and file a Restricted Application for benefits while the option is still available, you will receive benefits under the old rules even after the rules change.*

Do you think it might be an option for you? Then let's review the new rules about basic spousal benefits. If both you and your spouse have worked over the years, and if both of you have applied, Social Security will look at both of your earnings histories before they pay a benefit to you. If it is more advantageous for you to receive your own benefit based on your own earnings record, that's the benefit they'll pay you. If it is more advantageous for you to receive a spousal benefit that is (a maximum of) 50 percent of what your spouse receives, then they will increase your benefit to equal that amount. Simple, right?

Well, there is a loophole. Nothing in the old rules prevented someone from applying for benefits, but *restricting their application to the spousal benefit.* What is the point of doing that? By telling the government that they are specifically applying only for a spousal benefit, it allows the claimant's own benefit to grow by the 8 percent raises (DRCs) while at the same time collecting up to $60,000 in extra benefits from Social Security!

Making the Strategy Work

All of the pieces have to fall exactly into place in order for this to work. At FRA, which is 66 for purposes of this book, the spouse wishing to Claim Now, Claim More Later must apply for benefits and specify that he is restricting his application to *spousal benefits*. In order for him to be eligible to receive spousal benefits, his spouse must have filed for benefits based on her own record, or have applied for and suspended her benefit under the old Apply and Suspend rules. The spousal benefit can be collected until he reaches age 70, at which point he can switch to his own benefit. Let's look at an example.

Mike and Mary are both 66 (FRA). They've both worked over their lifetimes, but Mike has always earned more money than Mary. Mike's PIA is $2,000 and Mary's PIA is $800. Mary, who was born before December 31, 1953, files for her own benefit of $800 at age 66 *even though it is less than the spousal benefit she'd be entitled to* if she applied based on Mike's earnings record. Mike also files for benefits, but not his own benefits – because that would cause him to lose out on his DRCs (8% per year increases). Instead, he *restricts* his application to his spousal benefits – since they're married, he's entitled to claim benefits on Mary's record just as she is entitled to claim on his. By restricting his application, he tells the Social Security office that he is applying only for whatever spousal benefit he's entitled to. This allows him to collect $400 (half of Mary's PIA) every month, without affecting his own benefit in any way.

Over the next four years, Mike collects a total of $19,200 in spousal benefits. When he turns 70, he *switches to his own benefit*, which has grown by the 8 percent raises (DRCs) and COLAs and is now $2,920 each month. But the good news doesn't stop there. Once Mike begins to collect benefits on his own record at age 70, Mary can request a spousal add-on that increases her $800 monthly benefit to a spousal benefit that is based on Mike's record. Her new spousal benefit amount is $1,000; half of Mike's PIA at his FRA. Mary's spousal benefit is not affected by Mike's DRCs—it is based on his PIA at FRA. If he dies before she does, though, she'll get the benefit of his DRCs because she will receive a survivor benefit in contrast to a spousal benefit (see the previous chapter for information on survivor benefits).

There's a subtle point here. The person who is filing the Restricted Application must be Full Retirement Age (FRA) or older. So let's change the scenario a little bit and assume Mike is 66 (his FRA) and collecting his own benefit, but that Mary is only 62. Mary isn't FRA – she's got four more years to go.

She will never be able to file a Restricted Application for spousal benefits because the strategy will be eliminated by the time she turns FRA. She can still apply for regular old spousal benefits without filing a Restricted Application, but if she does, it's a very bad move. Her check will be significantly reduced, and permanently, as we demonstrated in Chapter 3.

But suppose Mary is 67 – in her case, beyond her FRA – and hasn't yet filed for her own benefit because hers is the higher one (she always made more money than Mike) and she wants to earn those 8 percent raises every year. Should she look into filing a Restricted Application for spousal benefits based on Mike's record? Absolutely, because she was born prior to December 31, 1953. If so, she would be able to collect 50 percent of Mike's PIA (assuming that Mike has filed for his own benefit) until she turns age 70 – without negatively affecting her own benefit. It will continue to grow because of the Delayed Retirement Credits (DRCs) and COLAs until she is age 70, at which time Social Security will switch her to the higher benefit based on her own earnings.

How the Strategy Will Work in 2020

If you were born on or before December 31, 1953 – meaning that you were at least 62 on January 1, 2016 – and your spouse is either collecting benefits or filed an application under the old Apply and Suspend rules, you will be allowed to file a Restricted Application for spousal benefits when you reach FRA. If you were born after December 31, 1953, like me, you must resign yourself to knowing that you are plumb out of luck.

When the new law takes effect fully, you will not be allowed to choose which benefit you receive when you apply. If your own benefit is higher, that is the amount will receive. If your spousal benefit is higher, you'll receive the spousal benefit. If you aren't one of the lucky ones who were able to take advantage of this and the Apply and Suspend strategies, you should look for other ways to maximize your Social Security benefits. This includes investigating any spousal benefits that you might be entitled to, and the benefits of waiting until age 70 to apply in order to get those 8 percent raises (DRCs).

> *When the new law takes effect fully, you will not be allowed to choose which benefit you receive when you apply. If your own benefit is higher, that is the amount you will receive. If your spousal benefit is higher, you'll receive the spousal benefit.*

CHAPTER 6

The Synergy of Roth Conversions and the Timing of Social Security Benefits

I am a strong proponent of Roth IRA conversions and, in fact, I authored the first peer-reviewed article on the topic that was published in **The Tax Adviser** (May 1998). Back then, few professionals could even grasp the potential benefits of the strategy, but nowadays you would be hard-pressed to find an IRA expert who *couldn't* come up with a situation where a Roth IRA conversion would be a good idea. I have interviewed multiple IRA experts on my radio show, including Ed Slott, Natalie Choate, Bob Keebler, Paul Merriman, Elaine Floyd, Jonathan Clements, John Bledsoe, and others. (These shows are all available on my website, www.paytaxeslater.com). I also published a detailed analysis of Roth IRA conversions in my book, **The Roth Revolution, Pay Taxes Once and Never Again**.

For a free copy of **The Roth Revolution**, go to www.paytaxeslater.com/books or order a hard copy from Amazon. My plan is to write an updated book on how IRA owners should respond to the Tax Cuts and Jobs Act of 2017, and Roth IRA conversions will be the centerpiece of that book. To get an early notification for that book, please sign up at www.paytaxeslater.com.

Roth IRA conversions were already an important strategy before the Tax Cuts and Jobs Act of 2017. If you believe, as I do, that the lower tax rates implemented because of the tax reform are not permanent and will go up again, this might be a great window of opportunity for you to make a series of Roth IRA conversions at a lower tax rate. It is also critical to realize that the best financial strategies take both Social Security and Roth IRA conversions into consideration — they aren't two independent calculations. When the "number crunchers" in our office are trying to figure out the best strategies, they must consider the impact of your income from Social Security on their Roth conversion calculations, and the impact that Roth conversions may have on your Social Security. There is a synergy in optimizing plans for Roth conversions and timing Social Security benefits, all the while minimizing income taxes. What follows is a brief introduction to Roth IRA conversions, followed by a discussion of why the best results come from combining optimal Social Security strategies and a Roth IRA conversion strategy.

> *If you believe, as I do, that the lower tax rates implemented because of the tax reform are not permanent and will go up again, this might be a great window of opportunity for you to make a series of Roth IRA conversions at a lower tax rate.*

What is a Roth Conversion?

A Roth conversion involves transferring money from a tax-deferred traditional IRA account to a tax-free Roth IRA. Assuming your employer gives you the option, you can also convert a traditional 401(k) to a Roth 401(k). Under the current rules, there are no longer any income limitations on who is eligible to make a Roth conversion. The amount that you transfer to the Roth IRA will be taxed at the time of transfer, but all of the future growth on the money will be tax-free. And a series of well-timed Roth conversions, as you will see, can make a significant difference not only in your lifestyle during your retirement, but also in the amount and the value of your estate that will continue to grow tax-free well after you pass.

Should You Convert?

What follows is an example that shows whether or not it can make sense to do a Roth IRA conversion.

> *A series of well-timed Roth conversions, as you will see, can make a significant difference not only in your lifestyle during your retirement, but also in the amount and the value of your estate that will continue to grow tax-free well after you pass.*

The assumptions used for Figure 6 can be found on pages 99-100.

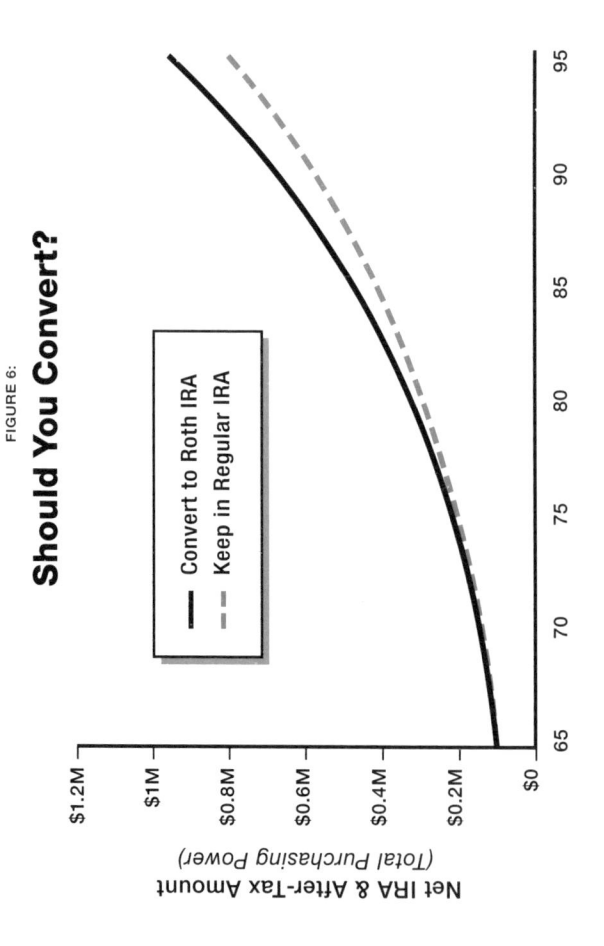

FIGURE 6:

Should You Convert?

Convert to Roth IRA
Keep in Regular IRA

Net IRA & After-Tax Amount
(Total Purchasing Power)

$1.2M
$1M
$0.8M
$0.6M
$0.4M
$0.2M
$0

65   70   75   80   85   90   95

Withdrawals from Traditional IRAs are taxable; withdrawals from Roth IRAs are generally tax-free. That's why, in order to do a fair comparison of the value of a Roth IRA and a Traditional IRA, you can't measure them by dollar amounts. You need to measure them in terms of a concept called *purchasing power*. Here's an example. If you are in a 25 percent tax bracket and make a $100,000 withdrawal from your Traditional IRA, you really only have $75,000 that you can spend – because you are going to have to send $25,000 to the IRS to cover the tax bill you will owe on your withdrawal. If you make the same $100,000 withdrawal from a Roth IRA, you can spend it all and not give a nickel to Uncle Sam. Figure 6 compares the value of the Roth IRA in terms of its purchasing power. And you can see that converting $100,000 of his Traditional IRA to a Roth IRA gave this client 18.5 percent more purchasing power in retirement.

Even though it doesn't show on Figure 6, under existing law, your children will get an even bigger benefit from your Roth IRA conversion. Under the old law, many if not most retirees between the ages of 62 and 70 could substantially increase their own and their children's wealth by making a series of Roth IRA conversions. The new law has changed the dynamic slightly. Because of the lower tax rates, we are now looking at executing bigger conversions before age 70, and also doing conversions even during the years when you will be required to take minimum distributions from your traditional IRAs.

Everyone's situation is different, and the decision about when and how much to convert must be analyzed on an individual basis. The best solution is to "run the numbers" for your own situation. Please see the back of the book for details on how we can help "run your numbers."

> *Under existing law, your children will get an even bigger benefit from your Roth IRA conversion.*

Why There is a Synergy between Optimizing Social Security and Roth IRA Conversions

Social Security benefits, for most people reading this book, are subject to federal income tax. The IRS considers your income from all sources, including but not limited to wages, interest (including tax-exempt interest), dividends, and pensions. To that income, they add one half of your Social Security benefit amount, and the total of those numbers is called your "combined income." If you are married and you file jointly, and the combined income on your tax return is greater than $32,000, then part of your Social Security will be taxed. How much will be taxed? That depends on your total income, but, as you might expect, the higher your income, the more of your Social Security that will be taxed. Generously, though, the IRS will not tax more than 85 percent of your benefit amount. The rate of tax, of course, depends on your own tax rate as well as a number of other factors.

How can you improve your retirement picture? By delaying your application for Social Security benefits for as long as you can – ideally, until age 70 – and by making a series of Roth IRA conversions between the years after you stop working and when you turn 70. Assuming that you stop working before you are 70, *your income will be lower*, and you can optimally execute higher Roth conversions while you are in a lower tax bracket.

Converting to a Roth While in Your Lowest Tax Bracket

What happens when you turn 70 ½? That's right – Required Minimum Distributions (RMDs). The government says you can't put off paying your taxes any longer and in most instances, they force you to take money out of your traditional tax-deferred retirement plans even if you'd rather save it for a rainy day. But the good news is that you aren't forced to take it out until you're 70 ½. And for most people, it makes more sense to leave your retirement money untouched for as long as possible – an idea I cover in detail in Chapter 4 of my book, **Retire Secure!** which, by the way, remains my flagship book.

*For a free copy of **Retire Secure!**, go to* www.paytaxeslater.com/books. *There you will find a list of my best-selling books.*

If you take my advice, you'll also wait until you are age 70 to start collecting Social Security checks. But suppose you stop working when you're 65? That means that, for about five years, you might have a window of opportunity when you'll have relatively little income. With no wages, no Social Security checks, and no RMDs, it might be a very good time to make a series of Roth IRA conversions. Executing a series of Roth conversions after you have stopped working, but before you begin to receive full Social Security benefits *and* before you start receiving your RMDs from your IRA will typically allow you to pay income taxes on the conversions at a lower rate than if you do them either while you are working, or after age 70 when you will have your highest Social Security income as well as the income from your RMDs.

Let's look at Peter and Brenda, who are both 66. Peter was able to apply for and suspend his own Social Security benefit by the deadline (the deadline has passed), and Brenda applied for a spousal benefit based on Peter's record even though he's not collecting his own right now. Then, they make a series of Roth IRA conversions starting at age 66 and continuing until age 69. Their taxable income is relatively low because there are no wages, just a small Social Security check for Brenda, and no RMDs from their Traditional IRAs. Since their income is temporarily low, their tax rate during these years is lower than it will be in the future, and the low tax rate will be favorable for Roth IRA conversions. Then, at age 70, their tax bracket goes up because Peter begins to receive his Social Security benefits—augmented by the four years of 8 percent raises. That means both spouses are now collecting Social Security and receiving RMDs from their Traditional IRAs, so they're suddenly in a higher income tax bracket. It won't be as favorable to make Roth IRA conversions now, so they stop.

As shown in Figure 2 on page 5, maximizing Roth IRA conversions and Social Security was the difference between worrying about money in your older years and dying broke versus living with financial security and dying with $2,013,881 when the other couple runs out of money.

Even though it might be better to make strategic Roth IRA conversions in your 60s when your income is at its lowest, Roth IRA conversions can still be advantageous for people in their 70s or older. I get asked that question a lot in my workshops, and I'll tell you briefly that there are many reasons why that's so – not the least of which is that conversions frequently benefit children and grandchildren far more than they can ever benefit you. Some people are not all that concerned about later generations because they are of the mindset that, after their deaths, their heirs should be grateful for whatever they get. "I paid for their braces. I paid for their college. Why should I go out of my way to help them after I die?" I am not saying there is anything wrong with that. We generally prefer a broader approach that often takes multiple generations into consideration. So, if a Roth conversion doesn't make a significant improvement during a client's own lifetime, but he will at least break even or realize a small benefit for executing one, we will frequently recommend that he bite the bullet and pay the taxes due simply because the conversion can make a life-changing difference for his heirs. But Roth conversions are an extremely complicated topic, and this little book is mainly about Social Security. If you want to learn more about Roth conversions, please sign up for early notification of my upcoming Roth IRA book by going to www.paytaxeslater.com.

The big picture, however, is that you must consider Roth IRA conversions *and* Social Security strategies to optimize your financial picture. They are not two independent calculations.

> *The big picture, however, is that you must consider Roth IRA conversions and Social Security strategies to optimize your financial picture. They are not two independent calculations.*

*For a free copy of **The Roth Revolution**, go to* www.paytaxeslater.com/books. *There you will find a list of my best-selling books.*

CHAPTER 7

What If I Have Already Made a Bad Decision?

In all probability, most readers have made some decisions that are good and some decisions that are not as good. Most of us can place ourselves squarely in clean-up mode. Clean-up mode is when you have made some mistakes in the past but are willing to correct the course if it isn't too late. If you have read this book and are now wondering if you made a mistake by not waiting to apply for Social Security benefits, it might be possible to stop receiving them. Let's look at your options.

If you change your mind within twelve months of applying for benefits, Social Security will allow you to withdraw your application completely. If you withdraw your application, your record will be treated as if you never applied in the first place – which may allow some people to use an even more beneficial filing strategy when they finally do apply. The downside to withdrawing your application is that you must repay all of the benefits that have been paid on your account to date – which includes your own benefit, spousal benefits, and benefits paid to children. Withdrawing your application can also affect Medicare, veteran's benefits, and railroad retirement benefits, but that's a very complicated discussion that is beyond the scope of this book. Anyone considering this option should consult with an expert in the area.

> *If you change your mind within twelve months of applying for benefits, Social Security will allow you to withdraw your application completely.*

But what happens if you've been collecting benefits for more than a year? Let's say that you started collecting benefits at age 62, and now, at age 67, you are reading this book and wishing that you had not applied as early as you did. Did you know that you can suspend your benefits simply by calling your local Social Security office? You must wait until your own Full Retirement Age to suspend benefits, but by stopping your Social Security benefits after you turn Full Retirement Age, you can earn an additional 8 percent per year plus COLAs, until you are 70. These raises, plus the COLAs you will continue to receive after you turn 70, will result in a higher benefit amount for both you and your surviving spouse, for the rest of your lives. And unlike the option where you withdraw your application completely, you do not have to repay the benefits that have already been paid on your record.

> *Did you know that you can suspend your benefits simply by calling your local Social Security office?*

What If I Am Already Receiving Social Security but I Like the Idea of a Roth Conversion?

What if you would like to consider a Roth conversion, but are already receiving benefits and are concerned that the increased income will cause your benefits to be taxed? You might be able to create your own perfect window of opportunity to do a Roth conversion, and get some of those 8 percent raises too, by suspending your benefits after you have applied!

And, bear with me here, suppose you have been receiving Social Security for less than a year but after reading this book you realize that you may not have made the right decision in applying for benefits so early. If you pay back the benefits you've received, you could get your Social Security strategy right (or at least better) and, without the income, you may be able to execute some Roth IRA conversions at a lower tax cost too.

> *You might be able to create your own perfect window of opportunity to do a Roth conversion, and get some of those 8 percent raises too, by suspending your benefits after you have applied!*

One word of caution, though. If you suspend your benefits after 4/29/16, any auxiliary benefits that are being paid on your record will also stop.

Returning benefits or changing benefits are supremely complicated topics that are well beyond the scope of this book. The point here is to just make you aware that, even if you have already filed, you may have options to change your decision that you might want to consider. So, please don't give up just because you did something in the past that you now regret. Seek out advice, and then move forward to a more financially secure retirement.

CHAPTER 8

Social Security for Divorcees and Singles

While this book was intended to provide information on the optimal Social Security options available for married couples, I'd be remiss if I didn't offer some ideas for single and divorced individuals too. So, let's cover those now.

Single People

If you have never married, your benefit will be based on your own work history, but there are still things that you can do to make sure that you get the most money you can from Social Security. This generally means waiting until age 70 to apply, so that your check is not reduced, and that you get those 8 percent raises and COLAs to boot. And I can hear the arguments already – "But what am I supposed to live on until I'm 70?"

It's a great question. The short answer is that you should consider spending your savings first – an idea that will raise many eyebrows, I'm sure – in exchange for getting a fatter guaranteed government check for the rest of your life. This is especially true because you don't have a spouse whose assets you might be able to rely on, in addition to your own, for support during your retirement. I don't have room in this little book to go into all of the details, but I do touch on this issue in Chapter 2. I also cover the topic thoroughly in Chapter 4 of my flagship book, *Retire Secure!* I encourage you to read it because it contains many important retirement planning concepts that are beyond the scope of this little book.

*For a free copy of **Retire Secure!**, go to* www.paytaxeslater.com/books. *There you will find a list of my best-selling books.*

As a single person, you may also benefit from taking advantage of some of the Roth IRA conversion strategies discussed in this book. In your case, the maximum dollar amount that you can profitably convert will be less than that of a married couple, because you use a different tax table.

Still not convinced? Then refer back to Figure 2 in the very first chapter of this book. Remember, the only difference between Couple Number 2 and Couple Number 3 were the elections they made with respect to Social Security and choosing to make Roth IRA conversions. Those two decisions made a significant difference in their financial positions thirty years later.

One final note for single people: if you are in a long-term, happy relationship but have never taken the steps to formalize it through marriage, you should know that there can be an enormous financial incentive for you to do so. If, for instance, one member of the couple has earned significantly less over time than the other, the lower earner will be able to collect more income from Social Security **if** he or she is eligible for a **spousal** benefit. That will improve total household income, benefitting you both. Perhaps more importantly, he or she may qualify for a survivor benefit that is larger than the benefit available based on his or her own earnings record —but only if *legally* married.

> *If you are in a long-term, happy relationship but have never taken the steps to formalize it through marriage, you should know that there can be an enormous financial incentive for you to do so.*

There are other reasons why marriage can be financially advantageous, but I don't have space in this book to cover them. If you are interested in learning more about them, please read my book, ***Live Gay, Retire Rich!*** (available at www.paytaxeslater.com/books). While I wrote it primarily to assist couples who were trying to navigate the ramifications of the legalization of same-sex marriage, the information contained within it is quite valuable to all unmarried, committed couples.

Divorced People

If you have worked, you can always apply for Social Security benefits based on your own earnings history. However, divorced individuals may also qualify for spousal benefits, but the rules are different than for married couples. Under the current rules, as long as you were married for at least 10 years, are at least 62 years old, and you are currently unmarried, you are eligible to apply for spousal benefits based on your ex-spouse's earnings history. (If you have remarried, any benefits you might be eligible for will generally be based on your current spouse's record unless your later marriage ended by annulment, divorce or death).

> *However, divorced individuals may also qualify for spousal benefits, but the rules are different than for married couples.*

After a woman who was attending one of my workshops realized she could collect benefits from her divorced spouse's work record, she spontaneously (if a little uncensored) blurted out, "Finally, the no-good S.O.B. is good for something." If you feel the same way, then you might not want to overlook the possibility of collecting benefits based on your former spouse's record. Your ex has to be at least 62 years old and eligible to receive Social Security benefits himself (or herself), in order for you to collect benefits on his or her record.

I can hear some wheels turning in some minds out there, so let's cover some of the more interesting applications of divorced spouse benefits. First, your ex-spouse will *not* be notified that you have applied for benefits based on his or her record. In fact, if your ex has FIVE former spouses, they can all collect divorced spouse benefits (assuming that they all meet the requirements) – and the strangest part is that nobody's benefit will be reduced because of it. Is this a great country or what? If your ex-spouse is eligible for benefits but has not yet applied – presumably because he or she is trying to earn DRCs – you can still receive spousal benefits if you have been divorced for at least two years. Remember, though, if you have remarried, any spousal benefit to which you are entitled will generally be based on the earnings record of your *current* spouse.

> *Your ex-spouse will not be notified that you have applied for benefits based on his or her record.*

Let's suppose that you do meet all of the requirements, and you are eligible for benefits based on the earnings record of a former spouse. What happens when your ex dies? Assuming that your marriage lasted at least ten years, you could be eligible for those survivor benefits we talked about in Chapter 4. And if your ex had multiple marriages, every one of his or her former spouses are potentially eligible for survivor benefits—along with his or her current spouse—and nobody's monthly check will be reduced! This assumes, of course, that they all individually meet the requirements to collect survivor benefits.

One point that divorced individuals should definitely not overlook is the possibility of filing a Restricted Application for spousal benefits. This could allow you to collect a spousal benefit from your ex, while at the same time allowing your own benefit to grow by those 8 percent raises and COLAs. Imagine the possibilities! You can take all that free money you got from Social Security thanks to that S.O.B. and go on vacation with it. In fact, why not send your ex a postcard and say that you're having the best time you ever had because of him?

> *One point that divorced individuals should definitely not overlook is the possibility of filing a Restricted Application for spousal benefits.*

As a divorced person, you may also benefit from taking advantage of some of the Roth IRA conversion strategies discussed in this book. In your case, the maximum dollar amount that you can profitably convert will be less than a married couple, but the idea might be important if there were children from your marriage. The benefits of conversions to children and grandchildren aren't discussed in detail in this book, but they're covered extensively in my book, ***The Roth Revolution***.

*For a free copy of **The Roth Revolution**, go to* www.paytaxeslater.com/books. *There you will find a list of my best-selling books.*

CHAPTER 9

Should the Question of Social Security's Solvency Motivate Me to Take Benefits as Soon as I Can?

One of the most frequent arguments I hear in favor of taking Social Security early is that the Social Security system will soon run out of money. And, if you don't take your benefits early, you will end up losing them. Of course, there is no guarantee that this will not happen. But let's look at the question from two perspectives: 1) the overall viability of the Social Security system, and 2) the viability of Social Security over your lifetime—even if you delay benefits.

First the conclusion, then the analysis. The problems facing Social Security's funding are real. Without significant changes, millennials and perhaps even Gen Xers might find it difficult to collect full benefits. But, it is unlikely that any changes will punish the current generation of 62 to 70-year-olds who choose to delay their application. Though there will inevitably be changes, and those changes could be detrimental, again, I don't think you would be hurt by waiting.

Let's look at the long-term viability of the Social Security system. No expert would say that the program is perfectly sound and nobody should worry at all. It's no secret why Social Security has significant long-term problems. As baby boomers continue to retire, stop paying into the program, and begin collecting benefits, the trust that funds the program will gradually deplete until it is in the red. One thing is clear, as it is currently structured, whether projecting 25 years ahead, or longer, measuring the program's "unfunded liabilities" (projected future benefits unmatched by the funds held in the Social Security trust fund), indicates that Social Security will not be able to deliver full-benefits to future recipients. That said, it is highly unlikely that the federal government will completely renege on its commitment to senior citizens. If for no other reason, it would not be politically feasible. What is much more likely is that Social Security's funding and benefits structures will be modified and renegotiated to prevent insolvency.

For example, when the program was struggling with what the Reagan Administration deemed a "financing crisis," Congress passed a set of adjustments to the system through the Social Security Reform Act of 1983. The changes enacted through that legislation went into effect *gradually*; for example, because of that 1983 reform, the Full Retirement

Age (FRA) will rise from 66 now to 67 in 2027. Future adjustments to benefits, such as slightly lowering cost of living adjustments or further modifying the retirement age, are inevitable, but there are two good reasons why you should not change your strategy because of potential changes if you are currently at or near retirement age.

1. Modifications to benefits tend to include provisions that prevent them from applying to the current generation of retirees. As Andy Landis, Social Security expert and author of *Social Security: The Inside Story* said in a recent article for CBS' Moneywatch, "nearly all reforms on the table will apply to younger generations, not those currently retiring."[1]

2. While reform is inevitable, that doesn't mean it will happen now or anytime soon. Short-term, Social Security has the funds required to operate at its current level for the next 16 years.

Given that, Social Security experts agree that Social Security's financial woes and/or the specter of future reform **should not** influence baby boomers' decisions about deferring or collecting benefits early. Larry Kotlikoff, co-author of the best-selling book, *Get What's Yours: The Revised Secrets to Maxing Out*

---

[1]   www.cbsnews.com/news/
      social-security-errors-that-can-cost-you-thousands

Your Social Security, and frequent contributor to PBS's Money Sen$e, recently published advice he gave to a woman born in 1960. In a nutshell, he told her that it is highly unlikely that benefit reductions will happen in time to have any effect on the benefits she will receive. Moreover, even if changes to the existing structure are passed, she and others her age or older will likely be grandfathered against any cuts to their benefits.[2] Likewise, Andy Landis urges people at or near retirement age to "calm down and follow your best plan for claiming Social Security benefits."[3]

Far from advising retirees to collect benefits now, experts are actively urging retirees to delay benefits. This January, the National Bureau of Economic Research released a working paper entitled "*The Power of Working Longer*[4]," which touts the benefits of deferring Social Security benefits. The working paper affirms the author's conclusion (drawn in an earlier collaborative working paper[5]) that for many retirees, collecting early is a boondoggle which can cost some of those families upwards of hundreds of thousands of dollars in lost benefits. On her web-

---

2   www.maximizemysocialsecurity.com/
     will-social-security-still-be-there
3   www.cbsnews.com/news/
     social-security-errors-that-can-cost-you-thousands
4   www.nber.org/papers/w24226
5   www.nber.org/papers/w22853

site, aimed at providing valuable information about Social Security to financial advisors, Elaine Floyd (a Social Security expert whose advice I highly respect) argues that now, with some new rules and deadlines going into effect this year (2018), and more changes on the horizon, it is an important time to provide "Boomers" with "good strategies for boosting their retirement income, including building delayed retirement credits."[6]

It's very likely that future benefit reductions will protect the additional benefits that accrue to people who defer taking benefits until at least age 70. Rather than reducing the delayed retirement credits that have already been earned by people at or above the FRA, future reform will likely further increase the FRA, effectively reducing the total value of the delayed retirement credits younger generations can accrue by waiting to take benefits until age 70. This is exactly what the 1983 change to the FRA for people born in or after 1960 effectively accomplishes, and further tinkering such as this is much more likely than an overhaul that would ruin the retirement plans of baby boomers.

In the face of Social Security's long-term solvency crisis, experts are still primarily focused on helping people avoid losing money by collecting early, or what I've termed "*The $214,000 Mistake*." This is

6   www.horsesmouth.com/mktgpage/social

because collecting early is detrimental to so many retirees and the specter of future tweaks to benefits is not nearly as threatening to their wallets as collecting benefits early. While people who are currently of or close to retirement age can probably avoid all uncertainty about Social Security's future by claiming early, **we know for certain** that claiming early can seriously jeopardize your financial future. [7]

---

7   Gary Koenig, Vice President of Financial Security at the AARP Public Policy Research Institute expressed a similar sentiment in this PBS article: www.pbs.org/newshour/economy/despite-decreased-benefits-many-americans-take-social-security-early

CONCLUSION AND SUMMARY

Here are the key points you need to remember about Social Security.

- If you apply at age 62, or as soon as you are eligible, your benefit amount starts lower and stays lower for the rest of your life.

- Cost of living adjustments magnify the benefits of delayed claiming, as well as the detriments of early claiming.

- Delaying your application for benefits becomes more advantageous the longer that you live.

- Since the surviving spouse will get the higher of the two benefits, it generally makes sense to plan for one benefit to be as high as possible. This can also be a game-changer for the surviving spouse.

- If you are married (or were married, but are now divorced), filing a Restricted Application for benefits could be a way for you to get more money from Social Security.

- Even if you started with one strategy, it doesn't necessarily mean that it is too late to make a change.

Here are the key points you need to remember about Roth IRA conversions.

- The 2017 tax reform reduced tax rates for many individuals. If you believe, as I do, that this reduction is temporary, then it may be beneficial to consider a series of Roth IRA conversions sooner than later.
- A series of Roth IRA conversions executed in conjunction with optimal Social Security strategies is a powerful combination.

Last but not least, don't leave these decisions up to guesswork. Guessing the wrong way could be very costly to both you and your heirs. The back of the book provides additional resources and ideas for personalized help.

---

*For more information about, and to request a free copy of our **upcoming companion audiobook**, visit:*
www.paytaxeslater.com/The214kMistake

APPENDIX

Use These Tips When Applying for Benefits

The following information deals with the mechanics of applying for Social Security benefits. It does not deal with Social Security claiming strategies discussed in this book.

Regardless of the method you plan to use to apply for Social Security benefits, you will need to gather information. The specific information you will need is unique to your own situation. The following is a list of information to consider:

- Your date and place of birth
- Your Social Security number
- The name, Social Security number and date of birth of your current and any former spouse
- The dates and places of your marriage(s) (if applicable)
- The dates of divorce or death of your spouse(s) (if applicable)
- Your citizenship status
- The month you want your retirement benefits to start
- If you are within 3 months of age 65, whether you want to enroll in Medical Insurance (Part B of Medicare)

The Application Process

Generally, there are three ways to apply for Social Security benefits: online, by telephone and in person at a Social Security Administration office. All three ways are not available in all situations. For instance, applications for divorced spouse benefits and survivor benefits must be made in person at a Social Security Administration office. Before deciding how you will apply for benefits, be sure to consider what ways are available to you, in light of the type of benefits you plan to claim.

Applying Online

To apply online, go to www.ssa.gov. Select "Online Services," then "Apply for Social Security Benefits." The next screen allows you to specify the type of benefit for which you are applying (Retirement or Spouse's benefits, Medicare or Disability). What follows is a series of screens with questions to be answered. The application does not need to be completed in one sitting. You can begin to complete it, save it and return to it later. After you begin to complete it, if you find that there is information you need to gather, it is best to save your application and return later, after you have gathered the missing information. This is because there is a time limit on how long each screen can be viewed. After 25 minutes of inactivity, you will be prompted to extend your time on that screen. You can extend it after the first two warnings, but after the third warning, there are no more extensions. If you don't move on to the next screen, all of the information you entered on that screen will be lost. There are also limits on what can be entered in certain fields. If you have entered a character that isn't permitted, you won't be able to continue to the next screen. You will get a prompt alerting you to the problem. Once you've fixed it, you will be able to continue. You will get a chance to review your answers, and you can go back and make corrections as needed.

Most of the questions are self-explanatory but in the past, questions like these have caused our clients some confusion:

> Do you want benefits to start in [current month]? / What date should benefits start?

These questions are to (1) establish what date you were first eligible to apply for benefits and (2) if you are applying after you were eligible, whether you want retroactive benefits. Up to 6 months of retroactive benefits can be requested. When considering whether you want retroactive benefits, make sure you were eligible on the retroactive date, and there aren't any negative consequences to making the application retroactive. (Example: Assume your Full

Retirement Age is 66, and that you are applying for benefits on your 66th birthday. If you ask for retroactive benefits, that means you've applied before your Full Retirement Age, and your benefit will be permanently reduced). If you are already more than 6 months beyond your Full Retirement Age, you can use a date that is 6 months before the date you fill out your application. This will give you six months of retroactive benefits, without your application being "early" or triggering a permanent reduction in your benefits.

Filing a Restricted Application for Spousal Benefits

This section applies to those of you who are among the limited number of married people grandfathered under the Bipartisan Budget Act of 2015 and are still able to restrict your application to spousal benefits as described in Chapter 3.

If it is your intention to restrict your application to whatever spousal benefits that you might be entitled to, you need to answer "yes" to the question that looks something like this:

> If you are eligible for both retirement benefits… and spouse's benefits, do you want to delay retirement benefits?

Answering "yes" makes it clear that you want to delay any retirement benefits to which you might be entitled based on *your own* record.

Finalizing Your Application

At the end of the application, you will be asked to confirm that your answers are true. There are no paper forms to sign. Your click on the "Submit Now" button constitutes your signature on the application. You will get an electronic receipt which identifies the Social Security Administration office to which your application has been assigned, with a confirmation number. You should print the receipt and keep it for your records. You can use the confirmation number to check the status of your application, provided that there is one month or less until your benefits are scheduled to begin. Usually, no documentation is required to be submitted to the Social Security Administration but a representative might call for additional information or documentation, or with questions. Once you have provided everything necessary, your application will be processed and you will get a Determination Letter by US Mail – not email – that tells you how much your benefit will be. You should review the Determination Letter carefully to make sure it looks "right;" that is, the amount on the letter is the same as the benefit for which you applied and that the Social Security number of the worker on whose earnings record the benefit is based is correct. If something isn't right, you need to contact your local Social Security office immediately. The longer you allow the mistake to continue, the more difficult it is to get it fixed.

Applying by Telephone

To apply by telephone, you can call the Social Security Administration toll-free at 1-800-772-1213. You might have to wait a while before you are connected to a Social Security Administration representative, but he or she will complete an application for you. Be sure to have all of the information you need before placing the call. If you don't, you'll have to call back. Once you have provided everything necessary, your application will be processed and you will get a Determination Letter by US Mail. You should review the Determination Letter carefully to make sure it looks "right;" that is, the amount on the letter is the same as the benefit for which you applied and that the Social Security number of the worker on whose earnings record the benefit is based is correct. If something isn't right, you need to contact your local Social Security office immediately. The longer you allow the mistake to continue, the more difficult it is to get it fixed.

Applying in Person at a Social Security Administration Office

To apply in person at a Social Security Administration office, most (if not all) offices now require an appointment. Call the Social Security Administration at 1-800-772-1213. Note that this is a national toll free number. Telephone numbers for your local office are not generally available. The Social Security Administration does not appreciate people "shopping around" for the office they favor; they typically will make the appointment at the office they consider appropriate for your address. You can go to the Social Security Office Locator on the Social Security website, www.ssa.gov, and put in your zip code to see which office it would be. For those of you in the Pittsburgh area, the addresses of the offices are:

921 Penn Avenue
Pittsburgh, PA 15222

Suite 120, 650 Washington Road
Pittsburgh, PA 15228

6117 Penn Circle North
Pittsburgh, PA 15206

2nd Floor, 4 Allegheny Center
Pittsburgh, PA 15212

120 Merchant Street
Ambridge, PA 15003

80 Regina Drive
Cranberry, PA 16319

Suite 210, 400 Oxford Drive
Monroeville, PA 15146

The hours of operation for most Social Security Administration offices are 9:00 am to 4:00 pm on Monday, Tuesday, Thursday and Friday, and 9:00 am to 12:00 pm on Wednesday. The Social Security Administration representative will complete an application for you. Be sure to have all of the necessary information at hand before your appointment. If you don't, your application will be delayed. Once you have provided everything necessary, your application will be processed and you will get a Determination Letter by US Mail. You should review the Determination Letter carefully to make sure it looks "right;" that is, the amount on the letter is the same as the benefit for which you applied and that the Social Security number of the worker on whose earnings record the benefit is based is correct. If something isn't right, you need to contact your local Social Security office immediately. The longer you allow the mistake to continue, the more difficult it is to get it fixed.

Which Way Is Best?

Applying online requires access to a computer and a level of comfort with its use that many people do not have. It does, nevertheless, have the advantages of timeliness and convenience. You do not have to wait to be connected to a representative for a telephone application or to wait for an in-person appointment. Nor do you have to complete the application process in one sitting, in the event that you find that you don't have all of the information on hand that you thought you did. Also, if you complete the online application correctly, the possibility of human error by someone at the Social Security office is eliminated. Eliminating the intermediary does, though, eliminate the opportunity for someone who could be more knowledgeable than you to confirm that your intent is being understood and carried out. You are the person who is best able to weigh the advantages and disadvantages of the application methods available to you and choose the one that is best for you.

ASSUMPTIONS

Assumptions: The assumptions used in the Figures presented in this book are as follows:

Figure 1

1. Primary Insurance Amount (PIA) $3,000 at Full Retirement Age of 66
2. Earns four years of Delayed Retirement Credits at 8% until age 70
3. Cost of Living Adjustment (COLA) is 2.5% per year
4. Social Security proceeds invested into an account that earns 4%
5. Roth Conversions executed at 28% tax bracket

Figure 2

1. Primary Insurance Amount (PIA) $3,000 at Full Retirement Age of 66
2. Earns four years of Delayed Retirement Credits at 8% until age 70
3. COLA is 2.5% per year
4. Social Security proceeds invested into an account that earns 4%
5. Roth Conversions executed at 28% tax bracket

Figure 3

1. Primary Insurance Amount (PIA) $3,000 at Full Retirement Age of 66
2. Earns four years of Delayed Retirement Credits at 8% until Age 70
3. COLA is 2.5% per year
4. Social Security proceeds invested into an account that earns 4%

Figure 4

1. Both spouses born in 1956, and John is the higher earner
2. Social Security benefits are invested in an account that earns a 6% rate of return
3. John's Primary Insurance Amount at Full Retirement Age is $3,000/month

Figure 5

Assumptions thoroughly explained within Chapter 4.

Figure 6

1. 65-year-old with $100,000 regular IRA and $28,000 after-tax funds are available
2. $100,000 traditional IRA converted
3. 25% federal tax bracket on minimum distributions from regular IRA

4. 28% tax bracket for Roth conversion amount & taxes on total regular IRA balances for comparisons
5. Long-term investment strategy resulting in 8% rate of return
6. Takes only required minimum distributions, reinvested in after-tax funds
7. Measured in total purchasing power that subtracts accrued income taxes from traditional IRA

ADDITIONAL RESOURCES

7 More Ways We Can Help You
Get the Most Out of Your IRA

In *The $214,000 Mistake, How to Double Your Social Security and Maximize Your IRAs: Proven Strategies for Couples Ages 62-70*, you've seen some of our favorite strategies for living well, retiring securely, and passing your wealth on to your loved ones.

Here we offer **seven** additional resources for growing your retirement nest egg and keeping your money out of the taxman's hands:

1. Get a FREE Copy of *Retire Secure!* (list price $24.95)—The revised Third Edition of Jim Lange's best-selling book, *Retire Secure!*, goes into much greater detail on many of the topics covered in this little book. This 420-page deep dive will guide you to dozens of additional strategies for tax-smart retirement and estate planning. The detailed table of contents makes it easy to find just the information you are looking for. Download a free digital copy at www.paytaxeslater.com/books or secure a hard cover copy on www.amazon.com.

2. Get a FREE Copy of ***The Roth Revolution, Pay Taxes Once and Never Again*** (list price $19.95) – This is Jim's book dedicated exclusively to the topic of Roth IRAs and Roth IRA conversions. It offers an in-depth, yet imminently practical, analysis of all things Roth. If this little book piqued your interest in the tax-free world of Roth IRAs (and it should have), a full exploration of the subject is available—again with a good table of contents to guide your search. Please go to www.paytaxeslater.com/books and download a free digital copy or order a hard copy at www.amazon.com.

3. **Keep Abreast of Cutting-Edge Wealth Creation Strategies** – Be the first to know about important changes to the tax code, the economy, and other emerging threats to your retirement with a free subscription to our email newsletter. Please go to www.paytaxeslater.com/reader to sign up for updates, special reports, and additional communications geared specifically toward making your retirement now or, in the future, a comfortable and secure place to live your dreams.

4. **Free Admittance to Jim's VIP Workshops** – Jim offers illuminating, in-person consumer workshops on a monthly basis. It's a truly rare opportunity to ask questions and get specific,

custom-tailored advice from a nationally recognized expert. The intimate, invitation-only events take place in the greater Pittsburgh, PA area. Naturally, they fill up quickly, so if you are interested and available, we encourage you to sign up early. Please see our website, www.paytaxeslater.com, for details.

5. **Listen and Learn from Jim and Other Distinguished Experts – For Free**. Yes, Jim has a vast library of hundreds of hours of his classic radio show podcast, **The Lange Money Hour: Where *Smart* Money Talks**, originally recorded live on Pittsburgh's KQV 1410 AM. Jim's reputation as an IRA and retirement planning expert ensures top-tier guests from the financial and retirement planning world. Notables such as John Bogle, Jonathan Clements, and Jane Bryant Quinn have been interviewed on Jim's show making for lively, informative and interesting discussions. All of our past broadcasts including both .mp3 audio files and transcripts are available on our radio show podcast archives web page which can be found at www.www.paytaxeslater.com/radio-show.

6. **Private In-Home Viewing and University of the Road** – We offer a number of DVDs and CDs of previously recorded workshops. These options are perfect for you if you do not live in west-

ern Pennsylvania but would like to upgrade your financial knowledge from the comfort of home. Jim makes it easy…simply throw a disc into your computer or DVD player to watch, or make the most of your time behind the wheel by popping an audio CD into the player and listening while you drive. Please go to www.jameslange.com for details.

7. **Free Second Opinion Consultation** – If you want a plan to retire securely and protect what you leave to your loved ones, we are scheduling a limited number of private meetings with potential new clients. Our *Free Second Opinion* consultations are reserved for those with at least $750,000 of investible assets. Please see the next section, **Everyone Needs a Good Financial Game Plan. Let's Find Yours,** for details.

Everyone Needs a Good
Financial Game Plan.

Let's Find *Yours*...

Our team of CPAs, estate attorneys, and money managers help our clients retire securely, cut taxes, and get the most out of what they've got. Then, we help them pass on whatever is left using strategies to minimize tax losses for their heirs.

Working ***as a team***, our CPAs, estate attorneys, and money managers optimize individualized plans and strategies for the benefit of our clients. Our CPA firm "runs the numbers," our law firm prepares wills and trusts[8], and we work closely with a low-cost index fund advisor who manages the money. "Running the numbers" provides an in-depth analysis of a client's options and possibilities: How much money can you afford to spend without worrying about running out of money? How much and when should you convert your IRAs to Roth IRAs? Does gifting make sense and if so, in what form, how much, and when? Additionally, we will recommend the best Social Security strategy for you.

---

8   Preparing wills, trusts, and IRA beneficiary designations is only available for Pennsylvania residents.

Furthermore, you will benefit by receiving a big-picture perspective. For instance, we may discover that a client who assumed he had to work an additional five years actually has sufficient funds to retire tomorrow. Or perhaps, he will choose to continue working, but on his own terms. Perhaps you and your spouse disagree over a move to Florida. Should you sell the family home and move or is it financially feasible to become snowbirds and get the best of both worlds? We can run the numbers and find out. Observations like these can and have been life-changing and liberating.

We do not manage investments internally at Lange Financial Group, LLC because we recognize that managing money is beyond the scope of our expertise. Just keeping our legal, tax, and number crunching capabilities is more than a full-time work for our entire staff. We decided to prioritize strengths. So, we looked for an investment advisory firm who brought the same kind of dedication and concentration to their field as we do to ours.

Happily, we found our primary collaborator, DiNuzzo Index Advisors, Inc., right in our backyard. They are a first-class organization that uses what we believe are the best low-cost index funds on the planet: Dimensional Fund Advisors. Individual investors can only access Dimensional's strategies through a select group of financial advisory firms, and DiNuzzo Index Advisors, Inc. is included in that select group. They have become our main resource when it comes to professionally managed portfolios for new clients. For clients who prefer an active money management style, we have a similar arrangement with our long-standing collaborators at Fort Pitt Capital Group, Inc.

P.J. DiNuzzo has put together a superb team of CFPs, ChFCs, CPAs, MBAs, and financial advisors, who have been serving their clients brilliantly since 1989. P.J. and his team are truly the hardest working group of financial advisors I know. Their process is in-depth and impressively client focused. It includes two to three meetings before they even agree to manage a client's money. An example of one of the strategies P.J. and his team use with our mutual clients is the DiNuzzo Money Bucket Stack Analysis™ (DMBSA). With this strategy, P.J. separates the client's investible assets into different accounts or "buckets" based on the time periods and purposes for which the client anticipates using those assets.

After P.J. and his team develop an investment plan, and our team develops a comprehensive retirement and estate plan, we help our mutual client implement the overarching plan. But our involvement doesn't end there. All good plans need to be modified and adjusted due to changing circumstances— portfolios increase and decrease because of market conditions, tax law changes, children marry, grand-children are born, and divorces happen. That's why clients meet with someone from our firm at least once on an annual basis to update their numbers, and with P.J.'s team on a semi-annual or annual basis to review portfolio performance. The DiNuzzo team also manages a client's portfolio using a best practice in the industry called "regular rebalancing."

When you become a client of Lange Financial Group, LLC, you benefit from the *integrated* experience of our financial professionals—all of whom have different but complementary expertise. In essence, you are getting what we think are the best retirement and estate planning strategies along with the best money management services that I am aware of for a combined fee of between 50 basis points (one-half of one percent of the money we actually manage) and 1% depending on how much money is invested.

We think this multidisciplinary approach is a win/win/win. It is a win for us because we get to do what we do best: implement our tax and estate planning strategies, help people retire securely, and wisely pass assets on. It is a win for DiNuzzo Index Advisors, Inc. because they get to do what they do best: manage money. **The biggest win, however, is for the client. You get our number crunching analysis, as well as comprehensive retirement and estate planning,**

and integrated money management using low-cost index funds all for one low fee of between 50 basis points and 1%.

We enjoy a 96% client retention rate with the mutual Lange/DiNuzzo clients, and our feedback indicates that our clients find excellent value in our combined services. It has been an interesting and rewarding journey for us, and we're working every day to make that journey even better for our clients.

We are proud of this success and would be happy to tell you more in person, should you qualify for a free consultation.

To inquire about a *Free Second Opinion** please:
Call 1-800-387-1129

Or visit: www.paytaxeslater.com/The214kMistake

*Free Second Opinion meetings are reserved for those with at least $750,000 of investible assets.

Notes

_____

_____

_____

_____

_____

_____

_____

_____

_____

_____

_____

_____

_____

_____

_____

_____

_____

James Lange